COFFEE WITH
JESUS

COFFEE WITH
JESUS

RICHARD W. BLOCK

ARPress
ILLUMINATING IDEAS.
EMPOWERING VOICES

ARPress
45 Dan Road Suite 5
Canton MA 02021

Hotline: 1(800) 220-7660
Fax: 1(855) 752-6001

Ordering Information:
Quantity sales. Special discounts are available on quantity purchases by corporations, associations, and others. For details, contact the publisher at the address above.

Printed in the United States of America.

ISBN-13:	Paperback	979-8-89389-570-4
	eBook	979-8-89389-571-1

Library of Congress Control Number: 2024920616

The picture of Jesus on the front of this book has little to do with Jesus himself, but it is all about the world his father created for us to explore, creating memories and learning experiences.

This book is actually volume two, a continuance of volume one, *Life as I lived it—Small Town Country Living*. The adventure continues.

Thank you for purchasing my book, which I know you will be able to relate to yourself the many stories and experiences within this book.

CONTENTS

ARMY BLANKET

Part of my gear that I always carry with me when I am on camping trips is a wool army blanket, among other things. You never know when it might get cold enough to need it. I keep a sheet and a poncho in the bottom of my duffel bag as well, in case it gets too hot or too wet. Be prepared is the Boy Scout motto that I live by. I also have a plan B and sometimes a plan C when I know I am going to take a trip somewhere. In this particular instance, we had taken a group of Boy Scouts out West to New Mexico and Colorado. It was the middle of summer and was plenty hot, but if you are camping in the mountains in Colorado, it can tend to get very cold and that is where we were spending the one night during our trip. My wife and I were sharing the same tent sleeping on cots. It's usually warm when you first go to bed and I usually start out sleeping on top of my sleeping bag. Later on, as it gets cooler I get inside my sleeping bag. As it gets colder yet, I reach into my duffel bag and pull out my wool blanket and lay it on top of my sleeping bag. When it gets very cold, I get up and put the blanket inside of my sleeping bag and then crawl back into it. This is usually over a course of a few hours as the night progresses. I had reached the point where I needed to put the wool blanket inside of my sleeping bag because of the coldness and when I awoke to do this, I could hear my wife's teeth chattering. I asked her if she was cold? She stuttered yes that she was freezing and couldn't sleep. I told her to unzip her sleeping bag. She said no that it would just make her colder and more miserable. She didn't know what I had in mind. So I unzipped her sleeping bag and put my wool blanket inside to warm her up. After a little while her teeth quit chattering and she was getting warmer. It was then that she complained that she had to go to the restroom which was a good distance from the campsite. I told her to just go outside no one will be stirring at two in the morning. I don't know what the temperature was, but it was darn cold! I put on a few clothes and my hooded sweatshirt. She asked me where I was going? I said I'm wearing these to bed because I have given you my blanket and I am going to be the one freezing if I don't wear enough clothing to ward off the cold. From then on I had to make sure that she had a wool army blanket among her gear because if I didn't, mine would be missing from my duffel bag! Wool was always itchy to me when it touched my bare skin, but I learned to tolerate it. Wool is a great fabric, and it will keep you warm even when it is wet!

BAD DOG

I like to play a little joke once in a while, especially when I am at work. I used to keep a pile of fake dog poop in a McDonald's bag on my desk. When the boss would come and visit the workers in his company, he would bring his bulldog, George, with him, to visit everyone as well. Bulldogs are so ugly, but they can be so cute as well. George was always a girl magnet. Whenever he would come into the work area, all of the girls would make over him, petting him and hugging him. I would always warn the new girls that George would usually leave a little surprise gift behind when he left, so they had to be watchful, that they would not be the recipient of George's little surprise. While they were making over George, I would slip the pile of fake poop somewhere around their desk without them seeing me. After the boss and George left the work area, I would make the comment for everyone to check around their desk to make sure they wouldn't find one of George's surprises. Of course, one of the new girls would point out what she had just found by her desk chair. I told her it looks like George has struck again and that she should clean it up right away! Of course, I'm going to get this, "No way!"

reply from the lucky victim. Me, being the gentleman that I am, would volunteer to clean it up for her. I would make a big production out of it of course. I would get down on my hands and knees with a paper towel in hand and look it over closely. Then I would sniff it a little bit and say, "I wonder what he has been eating?" Then I'd look up to see the sour look on her face and try not to laugh. Then I would say, "It looks pretty solid. I think I can just pick it up with my fingers!" Then I would scoop it up with the paper towel and look at it closely while I'm sniffing it again! Then I'd say, "It looks like he's been eating some corn!" At that, the poor girl would look like she's going to vomit! Everyone would start laughing and tell her it's a joke, as I put the poop back into the McDonald's bag and sat it on my desk. Life's too short not to have fun!

BLACKBERRIES

Many years ago, I used to pick a lot of blackberries. I was a lot younger then and I could climb the hills with a lot less effort. A friend of mine's family-owned farm property on N. Hogan Rd. outside of Aurora Indiana. They raised crops in the lowlands and had cattle grazing in the high lands of their property. On top of the hill overlooking the Hogan Valley was the mother of all blackberry patches. I had happened upon it while squirrel hunting one year and made a point to get permission to pick the blackberries that grew there. Blackberries grow on a vine like plant with many sharp thorns that protect its fruit. It takes two years for a blackberry plant to mature and produce berries, so every other year they would produce a large crop of berries. The years in between always produced fewer berries. The cattle that grazed there made paths around and through some of the thinner parts of the giant blackberry patch. This made it nice for picking berries because you could reach them. In the thick parts of the patch, the berries were unreachable because of the thickness of the blackberry plants and all of their stickers. At times I would stand and gaze at the berries in the center of the patch knowing I would be unable to pick them but that's okay because it left berries for the birds and other animals to eat. I used to take two buckets with me as I climbed the hill to the blackberry patch. Sometimes I would find a few stray plants and pick a few berries from them before I got to the main patch on top of the mountain. I usually had no problem filling both of my buckets once I reached the main patch and started picking the berries there. I took one of my friends with me and he could not believe the size of the blackberry patch. I had told him about it and he wouldn't believe me until he saw it! I had him bring two buckets as well and he filled both of them also. After that time he went with me every time I went to pick berries and we always filled our buckets. We had many good memories there picking berries. I would take my berries home and fill the buckets with water to get rid of any foreign particles and insects that may have been picked along with the berries. After the berries were washed, I would put them in plastic containers with a snap on lid after coating them with sugar to help preserve the berries while they are frozen. I dug a couple of these containers out of the freezer and took them on a camping trip with the Boy Scouts a while back. I made a cobbler in a Dutch oven with them. As the boys were enjoying the cobbler, I asked them how they liked it. They were gobbling it down and loving it! I then told them the berries in the cobbler they were eating, were older than they were! The date on the containers was 1989 and the berries were just as good as the day I froze them. This was the year 2015 so that meant the berries were 26 years old. By the way, I still have several more containers in the freezer. I'll get around to using them up someday!

BROKE DOWN MUSTANG

I worked as a maintenance supervisor for McDonald's of greater Cincinnati for many years and I operated from an office/warehouse in Harrison, Ohio. After leaving the office one morning, headed to one of our restaurants, I noticed a Ford Mustang sitting on the side of the interstate with its hood raised. I could see that it was from out of state, because it had an Indiana license plate on it. I usually kept a good inventory of parts in our warehouse and in my van, but today the parts I needed were in the warehouse, so I would have to make a trip back to the warehouse, to pick up what I needed. As I neared my exit on the interstate, I noticed the Mustang was still there with the hood up. There was a man and woman and two kids there, around the car. It had been several hours since I passed by there the first time and it was starting to get hot. It was a typical summer's day, temperature wise. As I returned from the warehouse on the interstate, I pulled up in front of the Mustang and stopped. As I walked up to the people standing by the Mustang I said, "You must be having a serious problem, because you have been here several hours." The man told me that they were from Indianapolis, on their way to Kings Island Amusement Park, when their car quit running and he pulled over to the side. He said that he had walked back to the local auto parts store and bought a fuel pump and put it on the engine, thinking that the fuel pump had failed, but that didn't seem to fix the problem. He told me that I was the only person that had stopped to offer help since he broke down there. I told him I was in the middle of a job and would be passing back this way in an hour or two and if he was still there, I would stop again and we would do something about his car. An hour or so later I returned to find them still there, so I crossed over the interstate and pulled in front of the Mustang once more. He told me that he still had no luck trying to get the car to start. I told him to climb into my van and we would go to the next town ahead and look for a repair garage. He asked if his family could come along, because he did not want to leave them there. I could see the sweltering heat was taking a toll on them. They were sweating and miserable, so I told them they could come also and cool off in my air-conditioned van. We went to the town ahead, only to discover the repair garage there, had gone out of business. I knew there was a repair garage that was open, behind where their car was, in Harrison, so we returned to the Mustang. I asked him if he had ever been towed on the end of tow chain? He told me that he had never done that before. I told him it's like playing tug-of-war. The object is to keep the chain tight between us. The way it works is, I have the motor and you have the brakes. I pull us and you stop us. Don't let me pull you faster than 35 mph, because it can hurt your transmission when your engine is not running. I hooked the chain up to him from my van and towed him to the repair garage. His family rode in my van for safety purposes. I told him that I knew the man that ran the repair shop and that he would probably have no trouble figuring out what was wrong with his car. The man offered to pay me for my help, but I told him, there was no way he could pay me for a favor. I have had people help me in the same manner and I am just paying it forward. After I left, I got to thinking about a Ford Pinto that I once owned. It used to break down in that same manner. It dawned on me, that his problem was, his timing chain had jumped a notch and disrupted the timing of the spark plugs firing, that's why the engine sputtered but would not start. I hated my Ford Pinto!

BUILDING A FENCE

My neighbor Rick, who lived across the street, came over to me one day and said, "Guess what, I bought another house that has a full basement, a two-car garage and a big yard!" "That's great, Rick," I told him. "What are you going to do with your old house?" I asked him. "I guess I'll sell it, I hadn't thought too much about it yet," he said. I asked, "How much are you going to sell it for?" At that point he said he didn't know but he would probably just sell it for what he owed on it, which was around $75,000. I made the remark, "Heck, I'd buy it for that amount!" His house was built on a single lot, but I knew it was appraised for around $105,000. Rick ordered one of those moving pods and it was delivered in his driveway. Rick and his wife began moving their belongings into the pod and it was soon ready to move to the new house location. A week or two after the pod was gone, Rick came to my house and informed me that he was all moved into his new house. It was then, that he asked me, if I was going to buy his house? I really did not want to buy his house, so I told him he should get a realtor and put it on the market and sell it to make a profit for himself, that he could spend on his new house. He told me that he did not want to put up with the hassle of selling the old house by way of a realtor. He then reminded me that I told him I would buy it. I asked, "Is the price still the same?" He said, "Yes, are you going to buy it or not?" Wow! Talk about putting the pressure on! I told him, "Well, I'm a man of my word, so I guess I will!" My wife and I had just paid off our house. Now we're going back into debt again! There was a lot of work to be done there after we bought it. Everything had to be painted because they were smokers. I also had to replace all the carpet. I put ceiling lights in all of the three bedrooms and switches on the walls, plus lights in the closets also. I installed a new ceramic tile floor in the kitchen and dining area. I had to buy a refrigerator and a washer and dryer. All of this renovation cost me about $5000. In the backyard stood and dilapidated wooden fence, that needed replaced. We had one just like it in our backyard and it needed replaced as well. The fence was rotten and falling down, but most of the posts were still in good shape and needed straightening up, with the exception of two rotten ones that had to be replaced. While I was in the backyard trimming one of the trees, the neighbor lady behind, came up to her side of the fence and asked me when I was going to fix this fence? I told her that where I come from, when a person builds a fence, the neighbor on the other side usually pays one half the cost. She asked me what I thought the cost would be and I told her six sections of premade fence at $35 per section would be the cost, but I do not have a truck to haul it here from Home Depot. She told me she could get a friend to haul it, but who was going to build it. I told her that I would put it up and she asked me when. I told her that I do my best work at night and some morning she would wake up and there would be a fence there! The next day we went to Home Depot and bought the fence sections. We both paid our half and loaded up the truck. We took it to my backyard, where we unloaded it and leaned it against a tree. A week or so later, I felt a little industrious one night, so I rigged up some work lights and installed the fence. A couple of weeks later, Charlie, the neighbor who lived behind me, asked me the same question about replacing the fence between us. I told him the same story that I told the lady across the street and he was agreeable, so we hopped into his truck and went to Home Depot to get the same amount of fence sections. When we told the employee what we wanted, he told us they were out of those fence sections for the season and would have no more until next year. As we were getting ready to leave, he said he might have some rejects on the lot, if we were interested in those. They were exactly what we needed and all they needed was a little repair! He made us a deal on everything there, for $100! We split the cost and I repaired the fence sections when we got them back home. Charlie worked long hours and he wanted to help me put the fence up, but I went ahead and installed it by myself after removing the old fence. Charlie came home as I was just finishing up. He felt bad because he hadn't helped me. I told him that it was okay. I just went ahead and did it on my own. I knew he always came home tired from work and didn't need to be doing something else. His health was not that good, so I thought I would give him a break. Sometimes you just have to take a little country tradition to the big city!

BUILDING A MOTOR COACH

H ave you ever wondered what it's like in one of those big motor coach buses that the celebrities travel in out on the road and how much one of those cost? Well, I'll answer those questions and many more. My old Boss and good friend, who was a multi-millionaire, owned several of them, but not at the same time. One of his first motor homes was a Bluebird and it was factory made to their specifications and you didn't have much say in how it was built or what luxuries were installed in it. After taking a trip or two in the Bluebird and having a few mishaps, he decided to move up to a bigger and better style of travel. This led him to a place in Angola, Indiana, where a man named Phil R. had a small company that built motor coaches for anyone who could afford one. Phil would buy a brand new stripped out M.C.I. bus from Motor Coach Industries in Roswell, New Mexico and drive it to his shop in Indiana. Then come the meetings and planning with the prospective new owner. This entailed every aspect, the same as building a house. A floor plan had to be laid out to begin. Kitchen or no kitchen, bedroom or lounge that turns into a bedroom and a bathroom with shower and sink are some decisions to make. Materials selection and colors and décor are in the mix. TV's and stereos need to be selected as well. Is this for personal pleasure or business usage? There are many factors that come into play that all depend on what the new owner has in mind of how he intends to use the coach when it's completed. His first M.C.I. motor coach cost $350,000. Just think of the House you could buy for that amount! It took me a long time to finally get all the bugs worked out of the coach and know that it would not have any problems on a long trip. He had that coach for a few years and then decided to trade it in on a newer, faster and bigger model. Here we go again! More planning and designing for the new M.C.I. coach. This one cost $650,000 and was made by Custom Coach in Columbus, Ohio where I saw Ray Charles and John Madden's coaches being built. Willie Nelson has 3 coaches for his group. I was back to square one, working out the bugs in a whole new coach. I always did most of the driving. Sometimes he would want to drive. It was his motor coach and everyone on board was in fear of their lives when he drove! He would drive all over and sometimes almost run cars off the road! We made some GREAT trips on those coaches over the years. I miss the people and the travel, but I don't miss the maintenance! Today a custom coach goes for around $1.3 million. You buy it and I'll drive it for you!

CHARLIE DANIELS CONCERT

A High School classmate of mine invited my wife and I to be guests at the Kentucky Speedway which her brother owned at the time, to watch the races and attend the concert that would be going on there at the same time. Charlie Daniels Band would be performing, and we would have VIP passes to attend everything. Who could pass an invitation like that up? Of course, we accepted! My wife and I rode with Nick and Judy, our hosts, to the Speedway in their car. It's nice to go with someone who knows the way and where to park up close. We went to the private booth overlooking the track where there were plenty of eats and drinks. We didn't stay there very long because the concert was getting ready to start and we were going to board Charlie Daniel's motor coach to meet him and receive an autographed picture of him as well as ask questions and get to know him a little. He has a great personality and a lot of patience when it comes to meeting and talking to people that are new to him. We got to sit on stage to his left and by the drummer, facing the crowd of fans. The band played all of their popular songs and we were right there in the middle of all the action. It was very interesting to see just how many timed Charlie would switch bows with a band member who stayed behind the drummer and would put a different bow in Charlie's hand every time Charlie put his hand behind his back with a frayed bow in it. Violin bows are made from horse tail hairs and tend to fray leaving broken strands to flail around in the air as it is moved back and forth across the strings. The band member would repair the bows as fast as he could by plucking the broken hair strands from the bows and having them ready for use as needed. After the concert ended, we returned to the private owners booth where Charlie joined everyone there for some eats and to watch the races for a while. It was a very enjoyable experience.

CHRISTMAS MORNING

When I was a youth, Santa Claus always came on Christmas eve and we always opened the presents he left us on Christmas Day. It was an exciting time for me because I could hardly sleep on that night. I lay awake waiting for my parents to come to bed. Our bedrooms were up stairs on the second floor and the Christmas tree and gifts were in the living room downstairs on the first floor in the front of the house. After everyone was settled and I was sure they were asleep, I would slip out of bed and quietly sneak down the stairs and past my sleeping grandmother whose bed was in the room at the foot of the steps. There I was on my hands and knees and sometimes crawling past my sleeping grandmother on my way to the living room where Santa had left all the goodies. I would very quietly open one of my favorite presents and begin to play. I hate staples. Why do companies always use those great big staples to hold a box of Army men and the stuff that comes with them so securely. It is really hard to open a box fastened in that manner without making a lot of noise. It never failed, someone would catch me in the middle of a battle and shoo me back to bed. For some reason I could go ahead and sleep the rest of the night. I guess I just needed reassurance that what I asked for was really there. I can still visualize those events as if it is unfolding right in front of me as I write this. I have always been blessed with a vivid imagination. Our daughter Janice is an avid shutterbug. With the advent of the digital camera, she takes hundreds of photographs and videos of everyone at Christmas time to preserve the memories any time we want to review them in the future. We never had that option back in the 1960s and very few photographs exist of the family and the joyous faces of our youth. I cannot count the many times that I wished I could go back and spend a few hours in that time era. Like the old Germans always used to say, "Too soon we get old and too late we get smart!"

CHRISTMAS PROGRAM

E very year, the First Baptist Church on Fourth Street in Aurora, hosted a Christmas program for the congregation and parents of the Sunday school classes. I think I was five years old this particular year and my class was to perform the song, Silent Night. We had been practicing the song every Sunday before the Christmas program so everyone knew it by heart. In the front of the Baptist Church was an elevated platform with a couple of steps and a knee-high railing on the front of it. Each Sunday school class would file onto the stage and perform their song or skit taking turns as their time came up. When our turn came, my class filed onto the stage to perform and I was in the middle of the kids as we were lined up. The lights shined bright on the stage area and the rest of the church where the people sat was dark or dimly lighted. As we started to sing Silent Night, I spied my mom and dad sitting among the people toward the back of the church. I stopped singing and started waving and shouting, there's my mom and dad. I think my parents were embarrassed, to say the least, so they did not react to my recognition. I thought to myself, maybe they don't see me, so I climbed over the railing, down the two steps and ran up the aisle to where they were seated. I do not remember what I said to them, but everyone was laughing and watching me as my mother told me to get back up there on the stage! I ran back up to the stage and climbed the two steps and then over the rail, back to my position among the class. I then resumed singing the rest of the song as everyone was still laughing. I couldn't quite figure out what was so funny? I thought the song went rather well!

CLAM CHOWDERS

My friend and employer was fond of touring the New England states in the fall, to see the trees turning into their fall colors. I would drive him and his family and sometimes a few of his invited guests and spend a week, just traveling around and seeing the sights there. The great thing about traveling around the East Coast is eating at the many restaurants which all serve freshly caught seafood. One trip I decided to compare the clam chowder that was served in each restaurant we dined at. I ate clam chowder once or twice every day and never had the same recipe twice. Every restaurant had its own recipe which differed from everyone else's. Even though every bowl of clam chowder was different, they were still very good. I can't say that I liked any one recipe better than another until the week we spent some time in Halifax, Nova Scotia. There was a little hotel named the Bluenose Hotel and it had its own restaurant which was run by a man and wife couple. He was the chef, and she was the maître d'. His clam chowder put everyone else's to shame. It was clearly heads above the rest! I ate it every day for one whole week and I could not get enough of it! My friend asked me one evening if I was getting tired of eating the clam chowder here every day? I said, "Absolutely not!" "If the chef is missing when we leave, it will be, because, I have kidnapped him, and I am taking him home with me!" He was an interesting chef. I talked with him about his clam chowder recipe and found out he only makes one serving at a time and not a kettle full, all at once. That has to be time-consuming, but that's the way he preferred to do it. His clam chowder had a distinctive yellow color to it, which implied to me, that he liked to put a lot of butter into his chowder. Since then, every time I order clam chowder in a restaurant and it does not have a yellow tint to it, I know to order some butter on the side and add it to the bowl of chowder. It does make a major improvement to any clam chowder recipe. Try this the next time you order clam chowder in a restaurant and you will be pleasingly surprised. I also add butter to the clam chowder I buy in a supermarket and comes in a can. Once you've had the best, it's hard to eat the rest, but butter helps, sometimes!

COMPUTERS

I avoided computers as long as I could, but my duties required me to get acquainted with and use a computer. As far as I am concerned, there is no one that can screw up a computer like I can! My abilities to use this piece of equipment are very limited. I have to learn as I go. It's like anything else. It's all trial and error. It seems I have to have someone come to my office weekly and try to straighten my computer out so I can continue using it. I upgraded from Windows 7 to Windows 10, and I have had nothing but trouble with my computer since I did that. Computers are a wonderful device, don't get me wrong, they are such a source of information that has no equal. I remember back in 1955, my father bought a complete set of Encyclopedia Britannica for me to learn from as I grew. I did use them occasionally for school projects and they were a great source of information. But as time went on the encyclopedias became outdated and lacked current events and history do to their age. After the advent of the computer and all of the easily obtained knowledge and information that are at your fingertips, those wonderful encyclopedias became obsolete and eventually done away with. It is totally awesome, the things a computer is capable of if you only know how to make it work. I enjoy the emails and different websites where I can find needed parts for pieces of equipment that I can find nowhere else. It is a great source of information especially if you need directions or diagrams that show you how to repair something or order parts for it. I worked with a couple of people whom I had do any computer work that I needed done in locating things for me that I needed on the job in the way of parts and information and diagrams. Since I have retired, I have to do those things for myself and I am pretty poor at it. Gosh I miss those people! I get by the best I can. I am no whiz by any means at typing. I had a program installed on my computer which prints everything that I say on the screen. It's called Dragon. It works great when it works. Somehow, I screwed it up and it quit working. My son-in-law Mark came over today and straightened it out for me. It is a really great program. I have to watch it closely because sometimes it will print something other than what I say because I did not say something clearly. I have to be careful to pronounce everything I say distinctly. It's like learning to talk all over again even though it is supposed to recognize the southern twang in my speech. One good thing that it does is that it makes me speak slowly so I am able to reread and correct any errors that the Dragon program might make. That way when I am finished writing a story, I have corrected any mistakes and proofread my story as well. This will save me a lot of time and trouble when I eventually submit my manuscript to my publisher. Someday I may master this darn computer, but I doubt it. There is just so much to learn!

CONCH SHELLS

When I am down in the Caribbean islands one of the prettiest seashells that I encounter is the conch shell. It is a rather large shell with a pinkish interior. If you cut the pointed end off and sanded smooth you can blow it like a horn. Sometimes when I go into a souvenir shop, they will have a lot of those conch shells sitting around. I like to go over and pick one up at random and blow it, then I will sit down and walk away to an area where I can see the conch shell that I have just blown sitting on the shelf. I like to watch the other customers who were observing me blowing the shell, walk over and look around to see if anyone is watching and they will pick it up and try to blow it themselves. Unless they know how to play a brass instrument such as a trumpet or a trombone, they usually have no luck in making any noise with it. After they get frustrated with trying to blow the shell, they put it down and walk away looking at other things on the shelves. I usually walk back over and pick up the same shell and blow it some more just to show them that it does make noise. Then I will put it back and walk away again. After seeing me blow it again the previous customer will usually come back and give it another try. Usually, they get the same result and can get no noise out of the shell. I'm usually chuckling at the frustrated look on their face and trying not to be too obvious that I am having a little fun at their expense. Often, they will come over to me and ask me, "What is the secret of making the shell below?" When I show them that you have to blow it like a trumpet it all makes sense to them and they are able to blow it. I have seen people by a conch shell and return it complaining that it is broken, and it won't play! Sometimes I have to show the employees how to blow the shell so they can show the customer how to blow it and that it is not broken. Most of all, I like to eat the conch that lives in the shell, especially when it is battered and deep-fried. It has a taste similar to shrimp. It is a common dish in the islands of the Caribbean and sometimes in the Florida Keys. It is not something you will readily find around the Cincinnati area. A couple of years ago the Boy Scouts were having a show and do program in one of the public parks and I took six conch shells there and lined them up on a table for one of the demonstrations. I thought this would be educational for the people attending the show and do program to learn how to blow the conch shells. The scouts had cooking demonstrations and samples to eat while other scouts were demonstrating not tying. There were displays to see and other activities all going on at the same time. I still think my conch shells were the highlight of the event because of the big sign I erected that said Sounds of the Sea, Blow Me! Every time I left my booth, a neighboring booth would hide my sign and I'd have to find it and put it back up. To this very day people still ask me if I'm going to do it again. What would you like?

CRUISES

A while back, a friend of mine Brett F. told me he was going to take a cruise with his family, and he had never been on a cruise before. This was his first time going on a cruise ship. He knew that I had been on several cruises before and wanted to know what it was like and if I had any advice for him. I told him honestly," It's all about the food!" He said he didn't understand what I was saying. And I told him the same thing again and that he would find out for himself once the ship got underway. I think he thought that I was pulling some kind of joke on him by the way he acted. Brett and his family were gone cruising for a week in the Bahamas stopping at this and that island and taking tours and seeing the sights. When Brett's family was aboard ship in the evenings, they attended programs that were put on by the staff of the ship. There was always something to do and something to see, but the highlight of the cruise was the variety and the quantity of the food available any time he and his family wanted to eat it. They were impressed with the variety of available seafood and his four-year-old daughter developed a great liking for lobster which is something she had never eaten before.

When Brett returned home, I asked him how he enjoyed the cruise and he said that I was right, "It's all about the food!" I asked him if he would like to take another cruise sometime and he replied with an emphatic, "Hell Yes!"

DAD'S WAR EXPERIENCES

My father was a soldier in World War II. He was in the 83rd division, which was a part of Patton's Third Army. There was a book written about his division, named the Thunderbolt across Europe. He was in the signal Corps and was always out front of the troops, stringing wire and keeping up communications. The 83rd division was known as the ragtag circus division, because they would put into use, any German vehicles that were serviceable and paint a star on them. My father did not like to talk about the war, and he said he would not take $1 million to go through it again, but would not take $1 million to have not gone through it. I think how lucky I am to be here, because he said he thought that he would never survive the war to make it back home. He was wounded three times and still remained to fight on. His lieutenant was killed in the landing craft as they landed on Omaha Beach. He was the first Sgt. and ran the outfit until the end of the war, with a Capt. being the next ranking officer over him. My dad did not like the captain because he was afraid to come up to the front lines and always stayed as far in the rear as he could. My father was a no-nonsense, serious man. He had our family's lethal temperament. It's a curse our family has always been stuck with and it's hard to suppress at times. I have to always take care not to lose my temper because of it. My dad told me he lost three jeeps in one week. When he called for a fourth one, the Sgt. at the motor pool, said he was coming up there to see what was going on. When he arrived, my father and his men were sitting behind a bombed-out farmhouse. The motor pool sergeant asked where the Jeep was and my father pointed to the field around the corner of the building, saying, that it was there in the middle of the field. The Sgt. asked what was wrong with it and dad said, "Nothing." "Go and check it out!" The Sgt. walked around the corner of the building, headed for the Jeep, when the MG 42 machine-gun on the opposite side of the field, opened fire! The Sgt. came crawling back around the corner of the building and said, "I'll send you another Jeep!" I asked my dad what happened to the Jeep that was sitting out there in the field and he said that the German shot it all to pieces and it caught fire and burned. My dad told me to never get a weapon with a scope on it, because someone always messes around with it behind your back. He told me he had just sited in, his 1903 Springfield with a scope on it and it was perfect. Later on, he was under attack by an enemy soldier, and he had to site down the side of his barrel to kill him, because someone has messed with his rifle when he was not around. Dad told me he also had no use for the colt 45 pistol that he was issued. He said he was stringing wire across a field one day, when a German lying on the other end of the field, shot at him. He said the bullet came so close to his head that it almost took his breath away! For some reason, the German jumped up and started running away. Dad said he took out his 45 pistol and shot all seven times at him, not touching him, and then threw the pistol at him for what good it had done him. After that episode he said he never had any use for the 45, even though he always carried it. The word was sent down that command needed prisoners for interrogation and would give one weeks pass in Paris for each prisoner. Dad and one of his men captured two German prisoners and he told his buddy to take them up to HQ and trade them for two passes. The prisoners never made it to HQ. The black soldiers in a grave's registration unit, grabbed them and killed them on their way there. One day, they were watching a dogfight between two fighter planes and the bullets were hitting everywhere on the ground. Dad noticed a man rolling around on the ground under a tree. He went over to see if the man might've been hit by a stray bullet and discovered that it was his chicken Capt. who was merely scared to death, but not shot. Dad had no respect for him, especially after that event. On one occasion, there was supposed to be a push across a river the following morning. Dad along with 30 men, were to cross the river the night before and set up communications. As dawn came, there was no push. The attack was called off and dad was not notified by his captain, of the change in plans. The captain hated my dad because he knew the feeling was mutual. When the Germans discovered the soldiers on their side of the river, it was almost a massacre. My dad and only three men made it back across the river in one piece. One night the captain called my dad and told him to come back and light his lantern for him, he could not get it to light! Dad simply told him, "No, I'm not going to do it!" "The captain said, "I'll have your stripes for this!" "Dad said, "Come up here and get them!" He never came, of course. Finally, the war ended. While dad was out and about, an officer came along and ordered his men to dig a latrine. When dad returned and saw what the men were doing, he told them to get some explosives and blow it, rather than spend all that energy digging it! After blowing the hole for the latrine, a Jeep with two MPs arrived, wanting to know what was the explosion about? He told them that they were ordered to dig a latrine and that's what they were doing. The MPs wanted to know who was in charge here. My dad told him that he was in charge. The MPs told him that he was in big trouble for using explosives and that he had to come with them to the Provost Marshall's office. While standing at attention, the provost marshal told him that the war was over, and these Germans are now our friends and that happenings like this could start it all over again! He said he was going to make an example of my dad and that he was going to be court-martialed! Dad laughed! The provost marshal looked puzzled and said that this was no laughing matter! Dad then told him to look out the windows and he would see what was so funny. When the provost marshal looked out the window, he saw that my dad's men, had set up machine guns and had the building surrounded! Then dad said," If I'm not out of here in five minutes, my men are going to level this place and waste everyone inside!" After saying that, he turned and walked away, leaving them standing there in disbelief! The provost marshal realized that these were combat veterans and were very serious men! Not a thing happened, and it was time to go home. On the train, a man passed through announcing that anyone caught with government property would be prosecuted. Most of the officers on board were still carrying their pistols on them. They were in disarray wondering what to do with them. My dad opened his duffel bag and said throw your guns in here. The train was crowded, and dad was using his duffel bag for a seat. As they came through and inspected, they never noticed his seat was a duffel bag. After the train arrived the officers wanted their pistols back. Dad said, "What pistols?" "I can get an MP to come over here and find them for you!" Needless to say, they didn't want them anymore. When dad arrived home, he had seven 45s in his duffel bag. He gave them away to friends, as he did most of the souvenirs, he sent home. I still have the German dagger that he took from a Luftwaffe Colonel that he gave away to a friend and was given to me after the friend died. I also still have the huge Nazi banner that he sent home, among other things. My dad passed away in 1967, only a year after I graduated high school. I regret that I never got to spend a lot of time with him. He was a great man and I can only hope that I have followed in his footsteps.

DECALS

D o you ever get decals that you really like and want to keep? The bad thing about decals is when you stick them onto something, they are permanently there and that's the end of them. If you want to move one, forget it! You will probably destroy it, trying to remove it and then it leaves a nasty spot on the surface of where it was removed from that you will have fun trying to clean off. When I get a decal that I would like to display without sticking it to the surface of something, I go to a sign store and buy some magnetic sheet material. I then take my sticker or decal and stick it onto the magnetic material. After making sure that it adhered securely, I can cut around it with a pair of scissors. Now I have a magnetic decal that I can put anywhere and move it around anytime and anywhere I want without destroying it! You can also do this with bumper stickers and put them on your car with no harm done to the painted surface! They are great for holding a note for a family member to the refrigerator door, for them to find when they come home. The magnetic stickers work well with shopping lists also. The uses of these magnets are only limited by the user's imagination!

The magnetic material is fairly cheap and easy to use. It is also a fun project for the children in the family. These projects help keep Mom's walls clean! "Look Mom! No more crayons on the walls, just magnets on the fridge!"

Do You Know?

1. What is the longest Interstate Highway in the U.S.?

2. What is the largest island in the Caribbean?

3. What was the hottest temperature ever recorded on earth and where was it?

4. What does the winner of the Indianapolis 500 drink after the race?

5. What's the most popular activity/sport played in the summer?

6. What U.S. city has the most lightning strikes per year?

7. What is the largest desert in the world?

8. How many states does Lake Michigan border?

9. What is the poorest U.S. state?

10. Where was the 1st public beach in the U.S.A. in 1895?

Answers:

1. I-90 Seattle to Boston 3,085.27 miles

2. Cuba

3. Death Valley, CA. 134F 57C

4. Milk

5. Biking

6. Clearwater, Florida

7. Antarctic Desert

8. 4, Michigan, Indiana, Illinois, Wisconsin

9. Mississippi

10. Revere Beach, Revere, MA.

DOGGIES

Here is a thought for all you dog lovers while you are walking your dog in the park on a nice sunny day. Have you ever tried picking a turd up by the clean end? Impossible isn't it!

DRIVE-IN MOVIES

I wonder how many drive-in movie theaters are still in operation today. The drive-in movie theater was a popular place to go, each time a new movie was introduced. I remember piling into a buddy's car with a bunch of friends and hiding in the trunk or on the floor in front of the rear seat, to sneak in for free while the driver and the front passenger paid to get in! You parked on a hump next to a post with a speaker on it. You rolled your window part way down and hung the speaker on it, you removed from the post. After you let everyone out of the car's trunk and off the floor, you headed for the snack bar to get some drinks and eats before the movie started. There would often be a group of cars parked together where everyone was friends or schoolmates. If you were alone with your girlfriend, you were usually making out in the backseat and didn't really see much of the movie! If you were with a group of guys, you were usually running around, harassing everyone else and having a good time doing that! That was a lot of fun and usually a standard for a Saturday nights adventure. In this day and age, I can only think of one drive-in movie theater still in operation. The speakers on a post are a thing of the past. You tune in the movie sound, on your radio, in your car. That eliminates driving away with the speaker attached and shattering your window glass or ripping the speaker wire, loose from the post! Now that I'm older, I prefer the nice, plush reclining seats in the heated and air-conditioned movie theaters with the 30 x 70' movie screen. Let's not forget the 3-D movies. Those were something that did not exist at the drive-in. Those were fun days for us, but hard for our grandchildren to visualize, when we speak of them!

EASTER

Easter is a great time of the year. When I was in grade school at Southside, we had a program that was called the Easter egg roll. All of the kids would bring colored, hard-boiled eggs to school with them for the event. We had a large, grassy hill behind our school, where we would roll the eggs down from the top to the bottom and if you got there first, without breaking your egg, you were the winter and you got a prize! All of the classes from grade 1 to 6 competed against one another. Some of the kids would throw their eggs instead of rolling them, just to see how big of a mess they could make on down the hill. Sometimes there would be contests to see how far and fast you could roll an egg with your nose. That was always fun to watch! Everything is different now days. Plastic eggs have taken the place of real eggs in most places. The standard game at Easter now, is the Easter egg hunt. My wife puts candy and coins in the plastic eggs, and we hide them in the backyard for the grandchildren to find. Each grandchild is assigned a certain colored egg to hunt, so they all get an equal amount of eggs to open. It eliminates the possibility of the bigger kids gathering up more of the eggs than the smaller kids, no more fighting and crying! I like to feed the squirrels in the wintertime, and I have a platform on my backyard fence where I put feed for the animals. One of the gray squirrels came calling just before the egg hunt began. My wife was looking out the window as we ate our Easter meal and noticed the squirrel was opening the blue eggs and eating the candy. It kind of made me wonder what colors a squirrel can see because he only opened the blue eggs and left the others alone. I used to find a plastic egg now and then when I mowed the grass for the first time in the spring. To avoid that, we count the eggs to make sure each kid finds all the eggs he is supposed to find, and grandma doesn't splatter one with the lawnmower!

ELECTRICAL PROBLEMS

A friend of mine, Kevin U. was building his own house. He bought one of those log cabin packages and was working on the inside wiring. I had used Kevin and two other talented carpenters to help me when I built my house. Kevin knew I was an electrician, among other things and he knew if he had a problem he couldn't contend with, he could call me for advice or a helping hand. To make a long story short, Kevin called me one day complaining that he couldn't get his stairway light to the basement to work. He said he tried everything and now needed my help in solving the problem. I stopped by his house with my tools and looked over his wiring. He had 2, 3-way switches, one at the top of the stairs and one at the bottom to turn the stair light on and off at either end and upon inspection, I verified that his wiring was correct and it should be working without question. I asked Kevin if he tried changing the light bulb and he said that he hadn't because it was a new bulb right out of the box. I told him to get me another bulb and that it didn't matter that the bulb in the light was new, it could still be a bad bulb right from the box. Kevin got another bulb from the same box and I switched them. I flipped on the switch and it worked fine. Kevin muttered, "Boy, do I feel stupid!" I told him, "Don't feel bad. I only had to drive 25 miles to change a light bulb for you!" Then we had a good laugh and drank a beer or two and everything was chalked up to just another day in the life.

FALLING DOWN

Have you ever fallen down and gotten hurt? Sometimes you think if you hadn't tried to catch yourself, you wouldn't have gotten hurt as bad as if you had just taken the fall without trying to catch yourself. My neighbor told me he had a nephew that was in epileptic and he suffered from epileptic fits and falls. He rarely got hurt because when he knew a fit was coming on and he was going to take a fall, he would just go ahead and plan the fall and turn it into a tumble that would cause him very little injury. I often thought how interesting that was. If you were quick enough, you could plan your fall and not get hurt very bad or even not at all. A friend of mine who worked for the phone company and spent a lot of time climbing telephone poles or standing on ladders, told me that the phone company had a climbing school for their employees where they were taught how to fall from different heights and land without great injury. I saw a 20 foot extension ladder be swept from beneath him one day while he was on top of it! After pulling a few wooden pole splinters out of his arms, he drank a Bud Light and was ready to go again! I think that was when he told me about learning how to fall and land safely. Most of the time when a person falls, they are on the ground before they realize it! It seems like your mind goes blank until you find yourself on the ground! I took a fall from the top of a 6 foot step ladder and I paid more attention to my not falling on the ladder when I hit the ground, then I did on the way that I landed. I wasn't quick enough to plan my landing on the ground. I landed flat on my rear in a sitting position, which caused a crushed vertebrae and broken disc in my back, which I eventually had operated on and it still causes me pain to this very day. At the time that I fell, I thought the worst thing that had happened was that I almost bit my tongue in half! All of the other complications came a little later. Nowadays I take more caution and stay focused on the task at hand so that I reduce my chances of falling. I can only advise everyone else to do the same or get someone else to do a task that is risky to one's own health because of age or health limits.

FEARS

I went to a Lenten dinner previously. It was a dinner for men from all the local churches covering many religions. There were a lot of people there and I knew most of them. It's always great to get together for some reason or another because I don't normally get to associate with many of them unless I run into them at Wal-Mart! And I don't go to Wal-Mart very often. They always serve a great meal at these get-togethers. After the meal is over, one of the local ministers or another official will give a talk on a subject of his choice. The topic of one of the speakers was Fears. He started out by asking everyone what they think their greatest fears are. Of course, the room grew silent while everyone was thinking about the question he asked. After a moment, the speaker said that most people do not fear death, but fear for the loved ones left behind to carry on after they die. Being the impulsive person that I am, I spoke right up and said, "My greatest fear is that the magazine on my weapon goes empty before the magazine on my enemy's weapon does!" After the laughter subsided, the speaker said he hadn't thought of that one!

FEDERAL FORCE PROTECTION SHOW

The Federal Force Protection Show is held yearly at Quantico Marine Base. Quantico is located south of Washington DC just off I- 95 in Virginia. It is a very interesting show where companies come from all over the world to sell their products to the government and military. It is a very high security show with all the latest technologies on display and demonstrated. Taking pictures is strictly forbidden and deadly force is authorized if someone is caught using a camera! Because of the product that the company I worked for manufactured, I was one of only three people authorized to have access to the runway with a vehicle. The Presidential helicopters are kept at Quantico. There are three of them, which are identical and are constantly landing and taking off after taxiing the length of the runway one by one and flying a circle to do it again. This they do all day long, so they are always prepared to fly to the White House on short notice and in record time! I had set times to do demonstrations out on the runway. But of course, it was a runway that was not in use and designated for demonstrations. When I wasn't putting on a demonstration, I would be working in our booth talking to various dignitaries and answering questions about our products which were tire deflating devices, used two flattened tires during high-speed chases by the police. When I had time I would go around to the other booths and see what each company had to offer. There were two other companies that were our competitors who also had booths. I would pick up some of their literature and bring it back to our company for our own observation. Our competitor's products were not as safe and as efficient as ours so we were not worried about their competition. There were many companies with many things to offer. One company offered a blast room. This was a room designed to be in the center of a building and be indestructible, where the employees could go to and lock themselves in, in case of a disaster. I often thought how many people could've been saved if there had been some blast rooms in the twin towers when they fell. The blast rooms would have survived intact among the rubble with survivors in them if they had only had some installed in the buildings and instructed the people how to use them. There were computer operated and remote activated guns. There were battlefield sensors that detected any kind of movement. There were companies offering bulletproof vests for individuals and dogs. There were companies that trained dogs for combat. I think I was the only one with a bicycle among my display gear that I would use it to get around from place to place when I needed to travel a distance at the show. I heard a lot of comments from different people saying that they wish they had thought to bring a bicycle as well. There was the latest in night vision technologies on display. It was one of the most interesting shows that I ever participated in. Now that I'm retired, I really miss going to and participating in those activities. It was a very learning experience.

FEEDING THE BIRDS

I enjoy having birds around my house as long as they're not making a nuisance of themselves. I provide feeders and birdhouses to keep them from clogging up my eaves troughs with their nests. Some types of birds like to build their own nests in the trees. Robbins always build their nests out of mud and grass and are very sturdy, resembling a soup bowl. Sometimes they will build them on top of a light fixture such as your porch light or in the rafters of your porch if they are exposed rafters. Doves do the same thing. Most of these birds fly south for the winter, with the exception of the starlings, sparrows and a few cardinals. Food gets very scarce for birds in the winter and that is why they migrate south to warmer weather and more abundant food. I use a variety of bird feeds in my feeders. I built a shelf type platform on my wooden backyard fence to put an assortment of other things like bread or leftover biscuits. I break them into small pieces so they are easy for the birds to eat. Occasionally, a squirrel or two will participate in the feast. One of the rewards I get from feeding the birds is that I get to clean the poop off of my cars! That is so much fun, you know! A bird is a funny animal. They have a sense of humor and they will poop on something, rather than nothing! It's a proven fact! I've often wondered how well birds can determine different colors. There are certain colors of vehicles they will poop on more often than they do others. Of course, let's not forget the human targets. I've cleaned my share of bird poop off myself, as well as off my cars! Sometimes I think feeding the birds is a big mistake. But it does make me feel good, knowing that by feeding them I am helping them to survive, especially in the harsh winter weather.

FISHING

ishing is an interesting sport. My father loved to fish and so did my mother. I, myself, really didn't have the patience to sit on a creek bank and wait for the fish to bite. It always seemed to be fairly easy to be able to catch the small fish like blue gills. I remember we used to go down to my Uncle Russell's barn and dig for fishing worms in his horse's manure pile. My father was more of an artificial lure person. He loved to troll for largemouth bass when he could find a good area that provided them. My neighbors used to set out trot lines and limb lines to catch any kind of fish they could and turtles also. At the end of the summer, the neighbors would get together, clean out their freezers and have a neighborhood cookout. There would be all kinds of fish and turtle meat plus a few squirrels and rabbits and also deer meat. It was always a fun time when all of the neighbors got together. When I got older and started to do a little traveling near and on the ocean, I found that fishing there was a total different experience. When you fish in the ocean, you do not have to wait for the fish to bite. The fish there are waiting for you to throw them the bait! Sometimes it's hard to cast out your line with the bait on it without a seagull grabbing it in midair and trying to fly away with it! It's a totally different kind of fishing when you are trying to reel in a seagull that is flying around in the sky, just so you can get him off your hook! One thing about fishing in the ocean is that you need to know when the tide is coming in and going out. The fish go with the tide. They come in with it and they go out with it, so most of your fish tackle shops have tide charts to help the fishermen catch more fish. The ocean waters can be so beautiful, unlike the muddy Creek waters back home. The ocean is so clear most of the time and the fish have no trouble seeing the bait. When you are fishing in the creek, you have to try different colored lures to find out which ones attract the fish. I'm always interested at looking at things from the other side of the fence. Usually when I am fishing with a friend, I will ask him if he has ever wondered what the fish is thinking when he sees the lure pass by him? I tell him the fish is probably thinking I'm going to grab that stupid lure and see if I can pull that idiot off the dock! The other fish are probably giggling as they watch old Charlie get dragged off and put on a stringer! It all boils down to the old saying, "some days you eat the bear and some days the bear eats you!"

FLAGS

I never realized the benefits of having a flagpole in my yard. The first flagpole I erected was at a friend's place in Michigan. I merely constructed it, just to put a flag on. I went into the woods and found a pine tree that was straight and tall and cut it down with my axe. After trimming the limbs from the tree, I took the bark off also. It looked like a piece of ivory. I took it back to the house and painted a finish on it, so it would not rot very quickly. I installed a pulley, rope and cleat on the pole and dug a hole with a post-hole digger and planted the pole in it. It stood for many years before rotting off at the bottom. The caretaker planted two posts on each side and put the pole back in place between them, using two long bolts through all three. This was a great idea! You could take one bolt out and pivot the flagpole down to the ground, if you needed to replace the rope or fix the pulley. From that time on whenever I erected a flagpole, I used that set up with the two posts and the pole in between. I did not realize when I put a flagpole in my yard at home, how often I would be using it for other things. By that, I mean, reading the weather. I find myself, looking at the American flag, several times a day to see what it is doing. It tells me how hard the wind is blowing and from which direction. It will tell if there is a storm brewing and if it is raining or if the sun is shining. The lifespan of the flags that I buy is usually around three months, before I need to replace them. I find that the printed flags float easier in the wind, than the embroidered flags will. It also makes a great landmark, because I have one of the few flagpoles in my neighborhood. Besides, I enjoy displaying my patriotism!

FLOWER

I bought a full-grown skunk at a pet shop. Her name was Flower. She was friendly to me and I had no trouble handling her when I took her places. Skunks are a night animal and are very active at that time of the day. One of the biggest mistakes that people make when they try to keep a skunk for a pet is that they turn it loose in their house like they would a cat or a dog. That is something you do not want to do because unlike a cat or a dog, a skunk will go and hide under the biggest piece of furniture or darkest place they can find. It is just a natural instinct of theirs to find a good hiding place. The best thing a skunk owner can do is to keep it in an open viewing cage where it can get used to being out in the open and override its instincts to hide all of the time. Skunks are a fairly fearless animal. They have three defenses that they use when they are approached by something such as a dog or another animal that they think might be a threat to them. First it will romp their front feet on the ground in a thumping manner. Second it will make a hissing sound. If that doesn't scare the intruder away, as a last resort they will use their scent glands to spray their obnoxious scent liquid at or on what-ever is threatening it. A skunk is also very nearsighted. If you see a family of skunks traveling in the wild, they are like one big ball of fur, all touching against one another, so they do not get lost from their family group. A skunk has a small head but a very large mouth like an alligator. One of a skunk's favorite foods is eggs. A skunk can pick up a full-sized chicken egg in its mouth and walk away with it. Chicken houses are a favorite hangout for wild skunks, which makes for an unhappy farmer as well as the chickens! I had a friend who owned a bar and I would take Flower with me frequently for a visit. I would put Flower on the bar while I sat with her and I drank a beer to to. She would quietly lay there as I stroked her soft fur. As people arrived at the bar, they would see her and come up to us to take a look. They would always ask does she bite? I would reply," Not if she likes you." Now Flower had her own little game she would play. She would wait for the person to stick their finger in front of her nose to see what she would do. She would sniff their finger a little and turn her head away as if everything was okay, but then she would snap her head back like lightning and grab the finger in her mouth, only pinching it, just to see how high the person would jump! All of the customers in the bar would be watching because they knew what was going to happen and to see how high and how quick the person would jump after being grabbed! The entire bar would be full of laughter at the person's reaction because they knew there was no harm done to him, just a surprise moves by the skunk. I guess even skunks like to have fun too!

FREDERICKSBURG

I was on my way to Quantico Marine base, to demonstrate a tire deflation product to members of the Pentagon, police, foreign dignitaries and military representatives. I was there early, so I thought I would take in some of the battlefield sites in Fredericksburg. As I returned to my company van from the welcome center, I noticed a puddle of antifreeze on the ground, coming from the front of my van. I returned inside and asked the man there, where I might be able to get a water pump put on my van. He said there was a shop just down the street where he gets all of his work done and they were pretty good about making repairs in a short time. I drove to the place he described and as I walked in I was greeted by a fluffy, brown dog that was very friendly. As I pet the dog, I thought how strange, I have a dog identical to him at home and his name is Bear. I told the men working on the cars in the garage that I have a dog just like this one. I asked, "What is his name?" One of the men said, "Bear." I thought to myself, you gotta be kidding! I asked if they would have time to replace the water pump on my van? One of the men, who happened to be the owner, told me that they could get to it tomorrow.

I said, "No, no, no." "I have to have this done today!" "I need this van to be on the Marine base at Quantico, in the morning, for demonstrations on the tarmac." "This van is only one of three that is authorized to be in that area." He told me that he could get to it in a couple of hours and that he would run me back home until it was finished, if I didn't want to wait around for that amount of time. I laughed and told him that I was from Indiana and it would be a long ride home. He thought that I was a local man, because we have a bit of a southern accent in southern Indiana. He asked me what was I going to do for a couple of hours? I told him that I was a master at killing time and it would be no problem. It was drizzling a little rain as I walked into the town of Fredericksburg. I passed a shop that was giving tours and had a half an hour film to watch before the tour began. I thought, well, that would take up some time. I went in and sat down. I watched their movie and got onto the tour bus. It reminded me of the kind of tour bus you would see in England. The driver gave the tour speech personally. It was not recorded and played over a speaker like some tours. He pointed out cannon balls that were embedded into pillars on buildings. He told the history of the battle that took place there. He pointed out bullet holes in different buildings and the stonewall the Confederates fired from behind at the advancing enemy forces. He told of the bridges that the Union forces were trying to build, while being fired upon by Confederate snipers and how the Union Army, brought up cannons to protect the bridge builders and silence the snipers. He told of how the union troops ransacked the city as they entered it. They were repelled at Marie Heights by the Confederate forces behind the stone wall. A general was killed there, while standing behind a building as a cannon ball passed through it, hitting him. After the tour, I spent some time in some of the shops before returning to the repair garage. When I walked in, the owner asked me what I had done for the last several hours. I told him about the tour and all of the things I had learned and seen. He said that he had lived there all of his life and never knew most of those things or saw them either! He said that he and his wife take walks into town every evening and that they would have to take the tour sometime. My van was done, I paid the bill, and I was on my way once more. Life is always an adventure, isn't it?

FRISKY THE SQUIRREL

One day while I was passing handbills to make money for the Boy Scouts, I encountered a baby fox squirrel as I was passing between houses. He was on the ground and jumped up on the side of a tree as I approached. I snuck up to the tree, reached around and grabbed him by the tail. I wasn't very far from home, so I hurried there and put him in a cage. After a day or two, my mother asked me what I was going to do with him. I told her I did not know and if she wanted him for a pet, she was welcome to have him. At that point, she took over his feeding and care duties and he became her pet. My mom had a way with animals and she and the squirrel became best of friends. Mom named the squirrel Frisky. Frisky had a cage in the living room but he was not always in it. Frisky had free run of the house most of the time. He liked to play a game where he would run into the corner of a room, jumping up and bouncing off of one wall onto the other and back to the floor where he would do it all over again creating a circle of movement. One day, I had a piece of cloth tied onto a piece of string that I was using to clean my shotgun. I noticed frisky was watching me in wonderment, especially the piece of cloth on the end of the string, so I laid it out on the floor, to see what he would do with it. It's funny how a squirrel will use its tail for different things. In this instance, he was sneaking up on the piece of cloth lying on the floor, with his tail cocked around beside him, to make himself look twice as big. Frisky was all stretched out and tensed up as he approached the piece of cloth. As he got as close as he dared, he started to sniff the piece of cloth and at that time, I gave it a jerk. When I did that, frisky jumped about 3 feet straight up into the air and landed several feet away. It was hilarious. Everyone was laughing. It was amazing how quick Frisky could move in the blink of an eye. When he slept at night, he would curl up and use his tail for a blanket. Mom gave him the best of care and spent a fortune on packages of walnuts at the grocery store. One of my favorite memories of him was, on a hot day, he would lie on a case of beer, in front of the fan, with his tail sticking up in the air like a flag, enjoying the breeze while he looked out the window, watching the cars go by or watching the television. For some reason, Frisky never had the desire to go outside of the house. Frisky was more of a family member than a pet. He was eight years old when he died and mom was heartbroken, we all were. Even after all these years have passed, I still think of him often and can visualize him enjoying himself, lying on that case of beer!

FROGS

My neighbor, Flash, stop by the house one day and asked me if I would like to come along with him down to the creek, to check the limb lines and the trot lines? I said, "Sure why not." "I'll row the boat while you check the lines." I have a nice sized fishing hole and camping area on my property which borders my lower fields. Several of my neighbors like to fish and lay out lines to catch fish and turtles. Sometime in the summer, the neighbors all get together and have a fish and turtle fry. A trot line is a long sturdy fishing line with multiple hooks, spaced every foot along the line, with bait on each hook. Liver or chicken chunks work well to catch catfish and turtles. Limb lines are just single lines with one hook, attached to a low hanging tree limb with bait on it. These work great for catching turtles because they have a spring like effect to them, much like a fishing pole, so the fish or turtle cannot break the line and get away. I can usually tell when one of the neighbors catches a turtle, because I will hear the crack of a 9 mm pistol, announcing their dislike of bringing a live snapping turtle into their boat. I told Flash to just let me strap on my pistol and I will be ready to go.

When we arrived at the fishing hole, I told Flash to get in the bow of the boat and I'll row him to the places he has his lines set out. I said to keep an eye out for snakes. They like to lie on low tree lambs hanging over the water and drop down on things passing beneath. I told him that as a joke, but low and behold, he spied a snake on an overhanging limb about 8 feet above the boat! I pulled my pistol and fired a shot. The snake fell from the tree, headless and dead as a door nail! I looked over at Flash, to see his reaction. He had his pistol in his hand and remarked, "I wasted my time pulling my gun out, didn't I?" I laughed and said, "Yep!" As we checked the lines, I heard a big bullfrog croaking up the creek bank aways. I asked Flash if he thought he could catch the frog, if I got the boat close enough to him? Flash said he thought that it would be a waste of time because we had no way of keeping the frog from getting away, once we got him in the boat. Usually, you have to put frogs into a bag or some container to keep them from getting away even if they have been gigged with a frog gig. I said, "That's no problem." "I'll just cold cock him." Flash said, "I've never seen or heard of that." I said, "If you can catch him, I will show you how to cold cock a frog!" I slowly rowed the boat close to the frog and flash grabbed him! He handed me the frog and said, "Okay, let's see you do it!" I put the frogs rear feet between my fingers and with a downward swinging motion, I smacked the back of the frog's head on the gun whale{edge} of the boat, killing him instantly! I then tossed the frog on the floor of the boat at Flash's feet. He said, "I'm going to catch another one because I can't believe what I just saw!" It always seemed I had to do everything twice, to make a believer out of him, but that's okay, we're like brothers and I don't mind.

FROZEN CHICKENS

In the early 1970s, the state of Indiana suffered a severe snow blizzard, and I was on my way traveling north to visit my relatives in Valparaiso, Indiana. It was three days after the blizzard and the highways were open again. As I traveled north, I saw plenty of large mounds of snow along the highway where the snow plow trucks had buried stranded vehicles of all types. I was north of Indianapolis a few miles when I could see dozens of vehicles parked along the interstate on both sides, much like you would see when people go to an auction. As I got closer, I could see a semi tractor trailer truck lying on its side in the middle of the median. Its rear doors had opened during the crash, spewing out its load as it slid on its side before coming to a stop. When the wind blew away enough of the snow to reveal its cargo of crates of frozen processed chickens, traffic on the highway stopped to help themselves. It was a calamity. People were on each end of some of the crates, pulling them back and forth like a tug of war contest, trying to get the crates away from one another! Others were grabbing the crates and dashing to their cars where they put them inside. People were slipping and sliding all around and falling down with crates of chickens in their arms! It was a free-for-all! I had to laugh! It was so funny to see all of these greedy people fighting over crates of frozen chickens! I was driving my Ford pickup truck that had a utility bed on it. I was fully loaded and had no more room to haul anything. I wasn't about to get involved in that mess anyhow. I often wondered how many people wound up with black eyes instead of crates of chickens!

GEODES

What is a geode? A geode is a round stone that looks like a head of cauliflower and can be found here in some areas of Indiana. They can be found in all sizes and if you break one open, you will discover that they are hollow inside and contain sparkling crystals, much like opening a miniature cave. Buck Crontz, my old scoutmaster, was in the habit of collecting geodes, to align his sidewalks and flowerbeds at his home. He liked to gather them up after the dirt and gravel roads had been graded by the County Hwy. Department in the Hoosier national forest, which is where our Boy Scout camp is located. One afternoon, Buck, myself and a few committee members, were traveling to the scout camp in Buck's car for a meeting and I was driving. As we traveled down the freshly graded road, Buck noticed a geode lying on the road that the grader had dug up. As we passed it by, Buck asked me why I did not stop. I said, "What for?" He told me that he collected geodes whenever he saw them, to decorate his home. I already knew that, but I thought I'd have a little fun with him. A little farther down the road, we passed up another geode. Buck said, "There's another one, why didn't you stop?" I said to him that he didn't need that one either because I was going to show him where the geodes grow. He sat quietly as we rode, probably wondering what I had just said to him. I turned into the driveway that led to the camp. I stopped the car a short distance down the driveway next to some stone pillars that were made entirely of geodes. Everyone asked me why I was stopping there and I told buck to get out of the car and follow me into the woods. After a short distance, I swept back the carpet of leaves uncovering hundreds of geodes lying there. I knew that this is where the workers deposited all the extra geodes that they did not use when they built the pillars. Buck could not believe his eyes! We filled the trunk of his car with dozens of geodes. The rear end of his car was so heavily weighted down, it resembled a motorboat on a lake with the front end sticking up in the air! That was the last time Buck ever stopped to pick up a geode alongside the road. I believe I broke him of the habit. He got his fill of geodes at last!

GIVING BLOOD

Several years ago, one of the ladies where I worked, decided our place of work, should have a blood drive. The Hoxworth Blood Center was called, and they arranged for their mobile blood van to come to our place of work and draw blood from any employee who wanted to participate. That was the first time I ever gave blood and that's what started my long history with the Hoxworth Blood Center. Ever since then, they call me every 8 weeks to please come and give my badly needed o-positive blood. Have you ever wondered what they do with the blood that they collect? Well, I'll tell you. First it is tested to see if it has any one of 39 contagious diseases. Then if it passes the test the blood is broken down into 3 separate things. 1. Platelets 2. Plasma 3. Red Blood Cells. Combined they formulate whole blood. O-negative is the universal blood. It can be given to anyone, but a person with O type blood can only receive O type blood back. It is important to know what type blood you have.

Here are the percentages of the population's blood types.

O type is 45% A type is 40% B type is 11% AB type is4%

I received a letter the other day from St. Elizabeth Hospital in Kentucky. It told me that they had used my blood to save a woman's life. That is the first time I ever received a notice like that. That letter gave me a sense of pride that I never had felt before! I am really glad that I could help a person in need.

GOOSE IN THE CRAPPER

We were on a trip in our troop bus to the Boy Scout National Jamboree at Fort A.P. Hill in Virginia and we were staying at a scout camp that was under construction and not open yet. We had plenty of room on our bus, so we invited some scouts from another troop to go with us to the jamboree. We had a long ride to the jamboree from our camp because the rule is that visiting scout troops are not allowed to camp within a 50-mile radius of the jamboree. We were lucky to find this place to camp. It was just on the fringe of the 50-mile limit. The property had been obtained from a contractor who went out of business. The property had a nice large lake and a very nice lodge type building. The Boy Scout Council there was in the process of constructing other buildings to complete the property as scout camp. There were no existing bathrooms for public use so the camp employed the use of a dozen port-o-lets which were lined up by the lake. They were very convenient because our campsite was across from them and within a short walking distance. There was plenty of wildlife to see and there were always Canadian geese there on the lake. One day we were getting ready to go and visit the jamboree so everyone was gathering around the bus in their class A-uniforms. The bus was conveniently parked near the port-o-lets so the boys could use them before boarding the bus. I had gone to my tent to get something from my pack when I noticed that I had a goose call in one of the pockets. I thought to myself, I might have a little fun with this, so I took it out and put it in my pocket for later use. As I headed to the bus, I thought I might use one of the crappers before I board the bus, just to play safe. While I was in there, I remembered the goose call in my pocket. I figured this would be a good time to have a little fun with it! I took the goose call out of my pocket and started squawking on it and at the same time pounding on and rocking the crapper back and forth as if there was a fight going on in it! After a short period, I stopped and listened to see if there was any reaction outside where the boys were gathered. It was funny, I didn't hear anything and I thought they must have gotten on the bus and didn't hear the commotion. When I opened the door to exit, I was surprised to see everyone gathered there to see what had taken place. It was so quiet you could hear a pin drop! I thought to myself, this is one of those moments and I have to grab it before it is lost! So I blurted out," I thought I'd never get that goose shoved down that round hole!" At that point everyone burst out laughing so hard that some of them were rolling around on the ground! After the laughter had subsided and we were getting ready to board the bus we noticed one of the boys was creeping up to the crapper to take a look inside. He carefully and quietly started to open the door to get a peek inside and I shouted," Look out!" "He's coming out of there!" The boy jumped back almost having a heart attack, again the laughter started all over again. I thought we would never get that bus loaded up! As I got close to the bus I overheard Brett, one of our scout leaders, telling one of the leaders of the other troop," We have something in our troop that you don't have, it's a Dick Block!"

GREAT AMERICAN BALLPARK

The great American Ballpark is in Cincinnati, the home of the Cincinnati Red Legs baseball team. At most of the home games they commonly have handouts. Different organizations can make money by handing out items at the entry gates before the game starts, as people file in. You have to have a group of at least 35 people to qualify for the job of giving handouts. We usually do this twice a year. We get all of our Boy Scouts and their parents to help out so we can make the quota. After all of the handouts are gone, we get to watch the ballgame for free as part of the program, plus, we get paid for our services! We load everyone up in our troop school bus and travel together. We bring soft drinks and snacks on the bus for everyone, as we travel to and from the game. It's a very fun time and it gives the parents an opportunity to meet and socialize with each other. It's amazing how many people come to the Reds game, just to get the handouts. Sometimes the handouts are hats, glasses, blankets, bobble head dolls of certain players or T-shirts. Some people come to watch the game, as you would expect, while others just come for the handout and leave. It seems like a waste of a ticket to me if you're not going to watch the game! Who knows? Sometimes they even win!!!!!!

GREEN SLIME

Somewhere back in the 1960s I joined the CB radio movement. I was fascinated by the CB radio that my uncle Leonard had in his home and his car and I just had to get the same equipment for myself. I first set up a base station radio with a super mag antenna on the roof of my home. I lived on a hill above the Ohio River, and I could talk to people many miles away because my radio waves would glance off the river giving me exceptional distance. The maximum range my radio license would allow was 150 miles and believe it or not I could easily talk that distance very easily. It wasn't like today where the radio frequencies are all jammed up with people talking on the same channel at the same time at different distances which keep everyone's radio transmissions from going very far. Nowadays you are lucky to talk seven or 8 miles down the road from your mobile radio in your car. But back in the mid-60s there were not that many radios blocking each other's radio waves. When I passed through Lawrenceburg, I always talked to a radio operator with the handle of Green Slime. I got to know many other radio operators in many different locations but I talked to Green Slime every day as I passed through his town. He was always there when I called and I thought to myself how can he always be there every time I call? It is funny how you can formulate an image of what the person you are talking to looks like in your mind and then when you meet them they are totally different than what you imagined them to be. Green Slime and I got to be pretty good friends over the radio waves. He always told me I should stop by his house sometime and meet everyone there being he lived only one block from the main highway that I traveled every day. One day I had a little time to spare so I told him I would stop by and we could eyeball each other. Eyeballing is a CB term for meeting each other. His house was easy to find because of the large CB antenna on the roof. I walked up to his door to knock on it but it opened as I got there by his mother who was expecting me and she told me Larry (his real name) was in the front room just go on in and see him. Larry was nothing like I expected him to be. Larry and his two brothers had polio when they were young and Larry got the worst of it and he was bedridden. Now I could see why he was always there! Larry was a year or two older than I, his brother Lanny was the same age as me and his brother Lenny was a couple years younger than Lanny. Larry spent his nights in an iron lung to help him breathe while he slept. He was a great guy and was always upbeat with a good sense of humor. He spent a lot time watching TV and his favorite show was Jeopardy. It's amazing how intelligent you can get from watching those kinds of programs every day. We became fast friends and so it was with his brothers and his parents. I became a family member and they were my family as well. We spent many good times together over the following years.

Larry's parents had a station wagon that was set up to haul Larry around in, safety belted down on a collapsible gurney. Lanny and I would load Larry up in the station wagon and we would drive out to the river bottoms where we would target practice with our pistols. I always teased Larry that some day he was going to shoot his big toe off if he wasn't careful because he always shot his pistol while lying on his back on the gurney! Larry was just as good a shot as any of the rest of us. It has been quite a few years since Larry passed on and I miss him dearly. He wasn't heavy he was my brother.

GROCERY SHOPPING

Have you ever noticed when you go to the Supermarket that whatever you went there to purchase is way in the back of the store? That's marketing strategy. They commonly stock the most sold items the farthest away from the front doors so you have to pass by other merchandise that you might be enticed to buy, thus increasing their sales. All supermarkets do this. Dairy products such as milk are a big seller as well as bread products. Think about it. Where are those items that you most use and where are they located in the store that you commonly shop at? Ever notice that the check-out person always asks if you found everything? I always reply that I have found too much! I came in here to get one item and then I had to go get a shopping cart to be able to carry everything! Then, my wife is always asking me what did I do with all my money when I tell her I'm about broke! Did you ever think about how much of your paycheck goes for food? I'm not just focusing on the supermarket but eating out as well. Restaurants and snack bars take a big bite out of your paycheck also. A few dollars here and a few dollars there, adds up! Just think how much money you would have if you didn't have to eat! I used to save a lot of money when I worked for a restaurant chain because my meals were free and I could eat all I wanted. It's a wonder I didn't get as fat as a hog, but you lose your appetite after eating the same foods every day. Let's not forget the coupons! There's a fortune to be saved if you know how to play the game! Don't you just hate to be in line behind a person that has an enormous amount of coupons?!!! After the clerk has that mess a figured out then it's time to write out a check or pay with a credit card that doesn't seem to not want to work right off! I was in the store the other day with my young son, and we happened upon a rather lady blocking one of the isles. HE pointed out how huge she was in no certain terms for everyone to hear and I told him that was not nice to say. Later on, we found ourselves behind her at the check-out counter. She evidently had a beeper in her pocket and when it went off, my son shouted, "Look out Dad, she's backing up!" Kids! What are you going to do with them?

GRUMPY

I am sure that everyone is familiar with Snow White and the seven dwarfs. One home in a well-to-do neighborhood had some full-size statues of the seven dwarfs in their yard. One day grumpy disappeared. He was just gone. No one had any idea where he disappeared to. All that was known about it is that he was missing. After a couple of weeks had gone by it was discovered that he was back! Where had he been for this period of time? Around Grumpy's neck was found a manila envelope attached by a string! Upon opening the envelope, it was discovered that there were all kinds of photographs. Guess what, Grumpy had been in Florida on spring break with a bunch of teenagers! There were all kinds of photographs of Grumpy and babes in bikinis on the beach and playing in the ocean. He was also seen riding around in a convertible with a bunch of bikini-clad babes having the time of his life apparently. Of course, at night time he was hanging out in the bars drinking and dancing with the rest of the crowd. After his return home, he was concreted permanently into the ground to keep him from getting into further trouble.

I would think that probably made him grumpier! What do you think?

HUMMINGBIRD

One spring day when we were at our cottage in Michigan I happen to see a hummingbird checking out the flower bed. I followed about previous years when we had hummingbird feeders hanging from the eaves of the house and how the hummingbirds use to flock around it drinking their fill of the nectar within the feeders. We usually never stayed here more than a couple of weeks at a time in the summer so there was no one around to refill the feeders when they went empty. I thought to myself, what the heck, I'm going to hunt up those feeders and fill them and re-hang them in the tree in the front yard. I searched around and found to feeders and filled them with the red nectar that the hummingbirds love so much. I really didn't expect the hummingbirds to come right away because I thought it would take them a while to notice the feeders and start using them. I was surprised to see two hummingbirds using the feeders that very afternoon! That was really amazing! I thought it would take them a couple of days to show up. The next day I noticed one of the feeders was empty. The caretaker was mowing the grass on his riding lawnmower and bumped the feeder with his head, which dumped all the red nectar on his head and down his neck coloring him red all over! "Gee! That's something I hadn't noticed before when I cut the grass the last time!" He remarked. I said," Well, I had just put it there yesterday." I left the golf cart sit out all night near one of the hummingbird feeders and when I went to use it, I discovered a hummingbird lying dead on the floor of the golf cart with his tongue sticking out. He must have hit the windshield like a kamikaze and killed himself. I gently picked him up and put him in a Ziploc bag which I put into the freezer to keep him from deteriorating. When we returned to our home in Cincinnati, I brought him with me to show the boys at the scout meeting on Monday night. They marveled at his bright colors and the shape of his tongue which was used to gather the pollen from the flowers and the feeder nectar. Then I returned him to the freezer once more to preserve him for exhibition at my next hunter safety class. I had 42 students in this particular class who passed him around and marveled at him and his Ziploc bag. I had invited the local Game Warden to attend the class and help out with the legal questions and test grading. I asked him after the class was over and we were packing up, what he thought about the hummingbird being part of the class demonstration. He said he thought that it was great but he had better take the hummingbird with him because it is a protected species. Oh no! Confiscated! And so ends another day in the classroom.

INDIAN FLUTE

Several years ago, I took an interest in the Indian flute. I am not a very musically inclined person, but I found the Indian flute can be played by anyone. Twice a year the National Muzzle Loading Rifle Association in Friendship, Indiana, holds its shooting competitions. There is also a large flea market in progress at the same time in conjunction with the shoot. There are all kinds of vendors at this particular flea market and one of them was a flute maker by the name of Jimmy Bear. Jimmy and his family make some of the finest Indian flutes available. In the wintertime he shops around for the finest wood samples at different lumber yards that are suitable for flute making. Jimmy's flutes can be very beautiful depending on the type of wood they are made from. The flutes are made in different sizes and different keys. I like the key of C personally. I would often stop by Jimmy's booth and listen to him play one of his flutes. I would ask him questions and he would give me advice about playing the flute. I learned that playing an Indian flute is a totally different method. When an Indian plays his flute, he is playing what he feels inside and not any particular made-up song. That's the great thing about playing an Indian flute. You are just expressing your feelings through musical notes. It is a very relaxing experience to be able to let your feelings go through musical notes. Jimmy's daughter plays the flute extremely well and sells recordings of her music playing. I like listening to other people play the flute because it gives me pointers on how to play mine. Everyone plays differently according to how they feel. Jimmy's flutes are costly because they are handmade and hand tuned to be perfect in every regard. Needless to say, I bought one of his flutes, but I do not play it as often as I would like. When I was out West on vacation, I stopped in a souvenir shop that had a variety of Indian flutes. I found a flute there that I liked and bought it. It is not as beautifully hand crafted as Jimmy's flutes are, but it is passable. Jimmy's daughter also makes cloth bags with a drawstring that specifically fit the flutes that they make. I bought two of the bags to keep my flutes in when I take them with me camping to play in the evenings. The only hard part about playing the flute is like anything else, finding the time to play it.

INGENUITY

W e take our Boy Scout troop to Michigan every three or four years to do a 50-mile canoeing trip down the AuSable River. We begin our canoeing trip in Grayling, Michigan. It takes us two days to do the trip. There are many businesses there, which offer canoe trips, rent you the equipment and pick you up at a designated point downriver when you are finished with your trip. We however, do our own hauling and the returning of our people and equipment ourselves. Most of the time, we would rent extra canoes because we had more people than canoes. There was a German couple that ran a canoe livery named, Carlisle. We always dealt with them because they were so friendly and would let us launch our canoes at their livery, along with the ones we rented from them. I had access to four canoes and the canoe trailer to haul them on, which meant we had to rent three more canoes to accommodate all of our scouts. On the first day out, we would travel about halfway down the river to Squirrel Bend Lodge, where we would spend the night and launch from there the following morning to finish the trip. I would drive the bus with the trailer behind to the pickup point at Parmalee and meet everyone there. The problem was, I had seven canoes to haul on a four-canoe trailer! As the canoes arrived at the pickup point, we loaded them on the trailer one at a time until the trailer was full. I thought to myself, I still have three more canoes to load up and no place to put them. After doing a little thinking, I grabbed my ax from the bus and slipped back into the woods a short distance. It was there that I found a maple sapling that I could cut down and trim the limbs off, leaving me a straight pole to work with. I cut the pole into four eight-foot lengths, which I carried out to the trailer, full of canoes. I laid two of the 8-foot lengths across the top two canoes and then sat two canoes on them. Then I laid the remaining two lengths on top of those two canoes and then put the seventh canoe in the middle, on top of them. After tying them all down, we were ready to head back to the Carlisle Canoe Livery and return their canoes. Gustav Preinel, the owner, was standing out front as we pulled in with our trailer load of canoes. He quickly ran back inside of his office, yelling for everyone to come outside and see how to put seven canoes on a four canoe trailer! I thought it was pretty funny that he got so excited over my ingenuity. He made all of his employees inspect the trailer load, so they would know how to improvise, if a situation would arise of similar circumstances. I hated to see Gustav and Christa retire and sell their business. I guess it's true that time stands still for no man.

JUMPER

M y wife and I and a couple of friends were returning from the Florida Keys. I was driving and I was making great time. The traffic was light and I was passing through Atlanta around 2 o'clock in the afternoon. I always wore a set of headphones and listened to the truckers on the CB radio, who would broadcast reports of any traffic problems to each other. I always left one side of the headset off of one ear, so I could listen to the conversation going on in the car. The headphones kept everyone else in the car from hearing the radio chatter, which annoyed them at times. As we started into Atlanta, going north on I-75, I received news from the truckers about a huge traffic jam that extended for miles on I-75. I thought, well, that's okay. I will just take the bypass and avoid that area. The bypass reconnects to I-75 on the north side of Atlanta, above the city, which I thought would be moving along normally. As we got a few miles from the junction, I found myself on the tail end of a several miles long, traffic jam! The chatter on the CB radio was informing everyone that there was a person on a bridge, which crosses the interstate, wanting to jump and commit suicide! The traffic was being held up from all directions. It was estimated there were 10,000 cars involved in the traffic jam! The truckers were asking each other if someone had a gun and if someone would shoot the jumper off the bridge, so they could get moving an again! It was hot and miserable, just sitting there and waiting. Everyone was yelling, jump, jump, jump, you ass hole! I thought to myself, that's only a highway viaduct and is probably only 15 to 20 feet above the pavement! What could he possibly do to himself at that height? Sprain an ankle or maybe break a leg! What a joke! He didn't have to commit suicide, because everyone sitting there in the miserable heat wanted to kill him! I think he finally fell and the cops took him away to jail with only a few cuts and bruises from the fall. It was well over an hour before we finally began moving again. It always seems that, no matter where you go, there's always some idiot, waiting to screw up your day!

LADIES WALLET

I was going to the dollar store one day and as I pulled in the parking lot, I saw something lying on the ground that looked like it might be a wallet. It was lying a couple of rows in front of me and I could still see it. I stepped from my van and walked over to see what it was. Sure enough, it was a ladies wallet that some woman must have dropped as she was getting into her car. I walked back to my car and sat behind the steering wheel as I gingerly picked through the wallet, looking for a phone number. The lady was a nurse and all of her credentials were in the wallet as well as her Driver's license, credit cards, Social Security card and money. There were other forms of important papers and receipts, but nowhere could I find a telephone number. I hate looking through other people's private possessions but I needed to find a phone number so I could return her wallet to her. I called the phone company information and asked for the phone number of the address that was on the driver's license. When I told the operator the lady's name, she said that person was not listed for that address and she would not give me the phone number. I thought I would probably leave the wallet at the local police station and let them deal with it. I was getting ready to go into the dollar store when a car pulled up and parked in the area where the wallet had been lying. A lady got out of the car and was looking all around before going into the store in front of her parking space. I watched as she came out of that store and went in the store next door. After a few moments she went into the dollar store. I looked at the picture on her driver's license, but I couldn't tell if it was her or not, in the picture. You know how those driver's license pictures turn out, they never looked like the person who is actually in the picture about half the time! I locked my car and went into the dollar store and saw the lady standing in line by the register. I went over and stood behind her in line. She was nervously looking around and was very restless. I said to her, "You look like a person who has lost something." She said, "Yes, I lost my wallet when I was here a while ago and I am hoping to find it." I said, "You must be Sarah." She said, "How do you know my name?" I said, "I have your wallet in my car!" A huge sigh of relief swept over her as she stood there. We talked as we walked out to my car and I told her about trying to find her phone number. She said she was divorced and lived with her mother and that is why her name did not show that she lived at that address. I told her to do herself a favor and make sure she has her phone number in her wallet, in several places. I told her everything was as she left it in her wallet and nothing will be missing or rearranged when she looks through it. I guess I have an honest face, because she said that it was okay, she trusted me, not even knowing me! I felt good that she got her wallet back and was happy again. I wonder how many people would have done the same if they had been in my shoes!

LIBRARY AND HISTORY

I n our small town of Aurora, we have the most fabulous branch of our main library. It is an old train depot building that has been remodeled and is a current branch of our library. There are different people who work there on different days. I like to go there on the days that Roy L. is working. He probably knows more about the history of Aurora than any living person today. I've known Roy for many years because we were Boy Scouts together. I don't know why he takes such an interest in our little town, but he is constantly searching for every little bit of history that he can find and make sure that it is recorded. They have programs on their computers at the library, where they can find anyone's family history that has lived in the area for generations. One day when I was there at The Depot, we looked up my family tree and I discovered that I was related to people that I have known for years and never knew I was related to them nor did they know they were related to me! I've always stated that when a family lives in an area for many generations you cannot help but be related to just about everybody! Family ties are forgotten as people pass on, unless they keep some kind of record for instance, like a Family Bible. People used to have a Family Bible where they kept all the records of births and marriages. I guess over the years, this practice has fallen by the wayside by changing times and habits coming into play. I remember my grandmother had a family Bible for her family, but I do not know what ever happened to it. Roy also looked up my great-grandfathers military record when he fought in the Civil War on the Union side. He was recorded to be in every major battle and survived the war to come home in one piece! There are thousands of photographs of our town's buildings, streets, people, steam locomotives, horses and buggies and old cars of every kind. A person could spend hours marveling at all the things there are to see there. Every time I go there to spend a few minutes, I wind up spending a few hours! I stopped in the other day just to say hi and Roy said I found something you ought to see. It was a newspaper article from back in 1945 that read, Richard Block dies suddenly. It went on to say that he was hunting with his son and suffered a heart attack. That was about my grandfather. I believe in Omens and this article has bothered me ever since he showed it to me. I am supposed to go on an Elk hunt with my son in Colorado this fall! Déjà vu or what?

LIFE IN THE 1950S

I grew up in a three-story house that was built in the early 1800s. Our only source of heat was a fuel oil heater which sat in a corner of our living room. Our cook stove in the kitchen operated on propane gas. The good thing about propane and fuel oil appliances is that if there is a power failure, it has no bearing on the operation of these appliances which were located on the first floor. In the wintertime, the heat would radiate into the upper stories. When it got too cold, we would light the oven on the kitchen cook stove and leave the oven door open for the heat to radiate out into the room. Our only source of water was at the kitchen sink. We always kept a large teakettle on the stove which supplied us with hot water because we had no water heater. This was fairly common in this time period. We had a galvanized washtub which hung on the wall at the foot of the steps which led up to the second story. When we wanted to take a bath, we would take the tub down from the wall and place it in front of the kitchen sink and fill it with a hose from the sink's faucet spout. We added boiling water at the same time from the teakettle to warm the bathwater up. We had no indoor bathroom. We had an outhouse located behind our house. That was okay in the summertime, but in the wintertime, it was too cold to go outside and use it. We had a thunder mug or pot as we would call it, for restroom use in the wintertime. The pot was a metal porcelain covered bucket with a lid and bail handle. We kept this behind the heating stove in the living room. After the plot was used, it was taken to the outhouse and emptied. By today's standards, I'm sure all of this sounds absurd, but that's the way it was back then and it is probably still a common practice in a lot of a remote areas where, "The sun don't shine" is a common phrase!

LOGGING

Dave S. Is a friend of mine who is a log buyer for a large company that has a sawmill. This has been his occupation for most of his life. I have learned a lot from Dave over the years that I have known him. I know that when trees grow to be very large, they mature. After a tree matures, it starts to hollow out in the center of the tree. It is at that point when a tree matures, it needs to be harvested. If it is not harvested it will continue to rot out in the center, which in time will make the tree worthless as lumber usage. Usually, timber buyers want trees to be at least 16 inches in diameter before they will consider harvesting them. One advantage of having mature trees harvested is that when the tree is removed it leaves a space for the sunlight to filter in and cause new growth to take the place of the harvested trees. Once a forest matures, it can become like a park, all nice and clean looking. That means poor habitat for ground dwelling animals. When trees are harvested, the sunlight filters in causing new growth it also creates a much richer habitat for the animals. Typically, loggers only take about the first 10 to 20 feet of the tree base, depending on where the tree limbs start protruding from the main base. Treetops are always left behind to rot in the woods. The rotting process enriches the soil to support the new growth. Treetops also provide firewood for people's homes. Firewood is another way to make profit from the logging process as well. Certain trees bring more money per board foot than other trees. It all depends on the demand for certain tree species. These demands change all the time. Tons of our American lumber is sold to foreign countries which has a bearing on the species and the demand quantities. A landowner needs to have a contract with the company harvesting the trees to ensure that there is no damage done to surrounding trees and grounds. Sometimes there large equipment can leave tire ruts in the forest floor and surrounding fields as they remove the harvested logs. Sometimes it pays for the landowner to contact a state Forrester and have him come to the property and evaluate the trees that need to be harvested to improve your forest. It is a common practice for the log buyer to mark the trees with spray paint so that you will know which ones are to be harvested and how tall the stump will be once the tree is cut down. Remember to establish property boundaries so adjoining properties will not be infringed upon. There is nothing worse than a neighbor complaining that some of the trees that were cut down were on his property! Sometimes there is a necessity to cut certain trees down even though they are not large enough to harvest. An example of this is the Emerald Ash Borer insect that infects and destroys ash trees. Because of this and other insects, most states prohibit firewood being transported to other states or even other counties within their own state. Remember, trees are a living thing and can be diseased or sick just like us.

LOST CANOE

I own several canoes and kept a couple on a canoe rack that I built in my backyard. Occasionally, my nephew Jim would call me and ask to borrow one for an afternoon canoeing trip down the Whitewater River. The Whitewater River can be dangerous at times and there have been many people drown in that river occasionally. He usually picked a calm time when it had not rained for a while and the river was not running so fast. I always stressed to him, the number one rule in canoeing is that you never let go of your paddle if you happen to tip over. Your paddle can save your life when it comes to climbing out of swift water or up steep muddy or slick banks. The paddle is also your only means of steering and propelling the boat! One Memorial Holiday, Jim and his son Matt borrowed one of my canoes for one of his frequent trips down the Whitewater River. I was at the Memorial Day service in our town's graveyard, when my phone rang. It was Jim and he said he had some bad news and some good news. He said the bad news is, I lost your canoe and the good news is we saved one paddle! I asked Jim who was the person that let go of his paddle and he said it was himself, in all the excitement! I asked him how can you lose a canoe? He then said that it sank and did not resurface! I said that canoe is unsinkable, how can you sink it? He said he didn't know and that they were lucky to be able to climb out of the river. I told him that as long as they were safe, that is all that matters! I can replace a canoe, but I can't replace my people! I told him once the service is over and I am back home, we will take another canoe and go down the river and he can show me what happened. Upon reaching the spot where the canoe went down, he told me they were trying to avoid a stump in the river and were swept into an area where a tree had fallen in the river on a curve with 10-foot-high banks. They used the fallen tree to be able to climb out of the river. He asked me if I thought the canoe was still down there somewhere and I told him yes, I believe the current has it pinned beneath the tree. We decided we would return the following day with ropes and a chainsaw to try and salvage the canoe. When we returned the following day, I lowered Jim down to the tree by rope and had him cut limbs and branches on the down river side, so the tree will break apart and hopefully the canoe might pop up. As we had planned, Jim started cutting the big limbs loose and they floated on downstream, widening the tree a little at a time with each cut. As chainsaws commonly do, it drowned out and stopped running after a while! As I looked out among the branches, I could see the nose of the canoe sticking up above the surface. It was standing on end! That's a 17-foot canoe standing on end! Jim swung out on his rope and tied another rope onto the canoe nose loop. He swung back to the top of the bank and I tied the canoe to a tree upstream. He asked me why I tied it off upstream instead of downstream and I told him that the current was going to help us pull the canoe out. Surprisingly the canoe came very easily out of the water and up the bank. We brought the one paddle with us and I launched the boat out into the river by myself and paddled downstream to a pickup point where Jim was waiting with his truck and we loaded it up for the trip home. Jim remarked that the next time he goes canoeing I'm going to have to go with him or he just won't go at all! Such is life.

LOST IN NEW YORK CITY

E very year the United States Military Academy at West Point New York, hosts a weekend camp out for the Boy Scouts in late April or early May. It is by invitation only and the invitation has to be applied for on their website in December. It helps to have a former member of your scout troop that is a cadet at the Academy, because you can use him to be your host. My son Richard was a cadet there and we used him as our host to attend several of their campouts. The cadets plan and run the activities which consist of military type competitions. I like to travel overnight, so we leave Thursday evening and get there Friday morning. This gives us time to tour the Academy grounds and the small town of Highland Falls, where they have great museums and souvenir shops. It takes 12 hours by Van or car and 16 hours by school bus to get from Cincinnati to West Point. We went a day early the last time we went because the leaders wanted to take the boys into New York City to see Ground Zero and some of the sights. We took the commuter train into Grand Central Station and then transferred to the subway which took us to Ground Zero. There were thousands of people on the streets, and I told the boys that even though they all look like Americans, they will hear different languages being spoken. It was a rainy day and there was a long line to get in to see Ground Zero which was all fenced in by plywood walls. As we stood in the waiting line, I saw a young man in a wheelchair handing out booklets in the rain that was steadily coming down. I gave my niece, Sarah, five dollars and told her to put it in his donation jar. After returning, I asked her if she knew why I had her do that. She said that she had no idea why. I told her it was because he was out there in the rain doing a job, trying to earn some money, instead of sitting at home collecting welfare. He simply deserved it. My wife asked me later on, if I saw Sarah put five dollars in the young man's jar and said that she was so proud of her for doing that! I said yes, I saw her and I'm proud also and said no more. After touring Ground Zero we stopped at Burger King for lunch. One of the boys had left his money on the bus and was trying to borrow some from the other boys to buy lunch with. One of the older boys, Tommy, was reaching for his wallet when I shoved five dollars into his hand and whispered to him to give the money to the boy. Later on my wife asked me if I had seen Tommy give the boy in need, five dollars to buy lunch with and she was so proud of him! I said yes that I was proud of him also and said no more again. We took the subway back to Ground Zero, which was an adventure in itself! Once there, we went out to the street to see the sights. We were only a few blocks away from the Empire State building and Times Square. I pointed out the small police station at Times Square, because it looked peculiar, sitting by itself, almost in the middle of the street! After we crossed a street intersection several blocks away, we decided to stop and count heads to make sure everyone was present. We discovered we were missing a 12-year-old scout named Kyle J. Some of the boys had been taking pictures with their cameras and cell phones and had a picture of Kyle with us as we crossed the intersection, so we knew he had to be here somewhere. Some of the adults backtracked looking everywhere for him but could not find him! Things were getting pretty intense at this time, so I told them all to stay where they were and I would find him. As I turned the corner I saw a police car parked at the curb. There was a major and a sergeant sitting in it. I went up to the major and told him I had a lost Boy Scout. I told him Kyle's name, age and what he was wearing. He had no cell phone or any money and disappeared five minutes prior when we crossed the street intersection ahead of their police car. The major put out a broadcast and called another car to assist me. When the police car arrived, it had two very attractive lady police officers, who asked for Kyle's description and then took me with them, driving around, looking for Kyle among the thousands of people on the streets. When we would stop at an intersection, the people would look through the rear seat window at me and point out that they had a white guy in there! I would act like I had handcuffs on and lip sync, help me! Just for them to see. I told the police officers that Kyle was a smart kid and that sooner or later he will go to a police officer somewhere and tell him he is lost. We decided to go to the train station to see if maybe he had gone there. As we arrived, the police radio announced that he had turned himself in at the small police station at Times Square! I called my wife who was with the rest of the group and told her I found Kyle and would meet them at the train station as soon as I could. You would have thought she had just won the lottery from the sounds of the cheering on the other end of the phone! There was also heard, a big sigh of relief. When Kyle came out to the police car, he was not the least afraid or shook up about getting separated from the group. He said he wasn't paying attention when he crossed the street and simply fell in with another group. I told him if he would have stayed where he was when he first discovered being separated, we would have found him right away! It took 2 hours instead! I told him he could run and he could hide, but I would find him anyway! Thank God for New York's finest!

MAKING GRAVY

My grandmother was a great cook, and I learned a few things from her about making gravy from the grease left in the frying pan after frying chicken. She always cooked everything in the white creamy Crisco that came in a can. The cooking oil that comes in a bottle, doesn't work out the same as the creamy stuff does. Grandmother always coated the pieces of chicken with flour and dropped them into the heated skillet that contained the melted Crisco. After the chicken finished cooking and was removed from the skillet, the grease with the chicken and flour residue in it was ready for making gravy. She would sprinkle a tablespoon of flour into the grease and stir in some milk, along with a little butter and some salt. The mixture would thicken into gravy in a very short time. I used to go down to the local supermarket after they butchered chickens and buy a dozen chicken necks. I would take the necks home and fry them up just to get the grease to make gravy in. I would make a batch of mashed potatoes to put the gravy on and I would be in hog heaven. I got to thinking one day about the different kinds of skillets our family used, so I thought I would do a little experimenting. I had a cast-iron skillet like my grandmother's, an aluminum skillet that was my mother's and a Teflon coated skillet of my own. I made a batch of gravy in each one after frying chicken in them, just to see if there was any difference in the taste. To my surprise, each skillet gave the gravy a little different flavor. They were all delicious nevertheless! For a long time, I would not let my wife touch the chicken grease because I wanted to make the gravy to suit myself! My wife is a great cook, but I still think I make the best gravy. Of course, that's just my own opinion. It tastes great on toast too!

MANUAL STICK SHIFT

I was 14 years old when I started driving the family car. It was a 1960 Plymouth with an automatic transmission. My grandmother drove a 1953 Chevrolet, three speed, manual stick shift, which was mounted on the steering wheel column. We called this, three on the tree. I wanted to know how to drive a stick shift car, so I asked my grandmother to teach me. Across the street from grandmother's house lies the city park. In the late 1800s, the city park was a horse racetrack. It had a circular raceway surrounding the center of the park. It was an ideal place to learn how to drive a stick shift. One day grandmother loaded me up in her car and took me across the street to the park. She stopped the car and slid across the seat to the passenger side while she told me to get behind the wheel. I did as she requested and then she began showing me how the gears and the clutch worked. After killing the motor several times while taking off, I quickly got the hang of shifting gears and going faster. It was easier than I thought it was going to be. All I needed was a little time and a lot of practice! Once I learned how to drive her car, I found that I could drive anything with a standard stick shift. Motorcycles were a little different, because the clutch was on the handlebars and you shifted with your foot. It was the same principle, just switched around backwards. I was 18 when grandmother traded in her old Chevrolet for a Nash Rambler, which was also a stick shift. She did not like automatic transmissions, so she stuck to her good old standard shift transmission type vehicle. I had a 1953 Willy's Jeep Overland wagon that I was driving at the time, so I went to the dealer and traded my Jeep for grandma's Chevy. When you renewed your driver's license at the age of 18, you were issued a permanent driver's license and you were not on a probation type license anymore. I had never gotten any traffic tickets until that time. Once I got that new permanent license it seemed like the cops followed me around and nailed me for anything they could! I never carried my driver's license on me, so none of the policeman who gave me tickets never got to see it! I always made them call the dispatcher on their radio and verify that I had a valid driver's license. It was a pain in the butt for the policeman, but what the heck, he is the one who pulled me over. I felt that he should work for the privilege of giving me a ticket! One day, I received a letter in the mail from the State of Indiana. It was notifying me that I had to meet with a state official from the Division of Motor Vehicles and bring with me, my driver's license for him to see. When I met with the state official, he asked to see my driver's license. As he stood there, looking at it, he said, "Do you know that you only have one point left on your driver's license and I can take it away from you right now?" At that point, I reached out and took my driver's license from his hand and said, "No you can't, you said I still have one point left!" At that moment, I turned and walked out the door, leaving him standing there! I had a friend, Thanny, who had a car body shop and painted cars. The old Chevy was white over green in color. I told him that I wanted it painted blue, top and bottom. The cops must've thought that I had vanished. There were still a few of those white over green 53 Chevy's running around town and they were watching them, thinking that one of them was probably me. I never received another traffic ticket in my pretty, blue, custom painted Chevrolet and I never changed my driving habits because there was nothing wrong with them! I don't know why, but I think they were just picking on me for who knows what reason. My friend who owned the local car dealership always serviced the police cars in his shop. I would stop by and look in the cruisers while they were getting serviced and read the top 10 list of people to keep an eye on that they always kept in their cars. I knew just about everyone on the list, including myself! I had to appear in traffic court once, for an unpaid parking ticket that I never received. They told me where my car was parked and at what time it was parked there when I got the ticket. I told them it was impossible unless someone stole it, parked it there and returned it to my place of work in the next town because that time slot was in the middle of my workday and I had the timecard to prove I was at work at that time and nowhere near that area! I never did figure that one out! They dismissed the charges. You think? Duh!

MARBLES

I was rummaging through some things I had stored away for many years and I came across this small wooden barrel. It was meant to be a bank because of the coin slot in the top. I had never used it for a bank, because I kept all my marbles in it and they were still in there! As I looked them over, they brought back fond memories of grade school and playing marbles behind the school in the graveled walkway. There were plenty of cat's eyes, crystals, clay marbles and steel marbles. We used to call the steel marbles, stealies. It was an everyday game for lots of kids in various grades. There were plenty of players carrying around their bags of marbles and challenging other players to a game of keeps at recess. When you play keeps, if you hit the other players marble you got to keep it! Another game we played was called pots. To play pots, a circle was drawn in the gravel with a stick and everyone contributed 2 or 3 marbles into the center of the circle or pot. You took turns trying to knock marbles from the circle with your favorite shooting marble. The marbles you knocked out of the circle, were yours to keep! Sometimes when you knocked one out, the marble you hit it with would stay inside the circle to become another marble to shoot at. I remember a girl in my class whose name was Francis Steele. She had a giant steel marble the size of a small cannonball. There was no way any player could knock it from the circle if she put it there. I remember seeing other player's marbles bounce off of it and sometimes shattering when they hit. It got to the point where no one would play marbles with her if she used it! I don't know why fun games like this and others, just fade away. I guess the computer video games and smart phones have created a different kind of fun! Batteries included, of course!

MOCKINGBIRD

Here in the suburbs of the big city of Cincinnati, we have plenty of streetlights the same as in any town or suburb. Sometimes those streetlights create an environment the same as daytime. For the last four or five years a Mockingbird has been sharing our neighborhood. He likes to sit by the streetlight in front of our house and sing all night. There are times when I think I'd like to go out there and shoot him down, just to get a good nights sleep. I can't help but wonder when he gets some sleep because he is out there singing in the daytime also. They don't call them a Mockingbird for nothing because they can repeat whatever they hear. Sometimes when I am outside working around the house, I will whistle some different tunes and he will sing them back to me. Sometimes I will imitate other birds and he will mock those sounds as well. Sometimes I think he tries to imitate the sounds of cars going by. He seems to know no limits when it comes to imitations. Sometimes I can hardly wait for wintertime to come so he will go south for the winter and give me some peace of mind! Sometimes he drives me nuts and I think that sometimes I am returning the favor! I guess it all boils down to the battle of the birdbrains. When springtime rolls around I wonder if he's coming back. He was late getting here this particular year and I was hoping that something happened to him on his way here. I heard him singing in the tree across the street the other day and I thought to myself, OH CRAP!!! HE'S BACK!!!!!

MOM'S HALLOWEEN CREATIONS

My mother was a very creative person. Her side of the family was very artistic, and her sister Mary went to college and majored in art. I guess that's where I inherited my artistic ability. In 1956 when I was eight years old, I joined the Cub Scouts. Cub Scouts was a popular organization at that time and I think one of the conditions that I got to join was that my mother had to be a den mother. She liked to make things out of papier-mâché and one of her projects was to build a giant shoe, which was to be a float in a parade. It was based on the poem, "There was an old woman who lived in a shoe who had so many children she didn't know what to do." Mom, with dad's help, built a shoe like frame out of wood and chicken wire. Mom and her den of Cub Scouts cut newspapers into strips. After mixing up a tub of wallpaper paste, the paper strips were dunked into the paste and then applied to the frame of the shoe. This is how papier-mâché is made. After coating the frame with the newspaper paste soaked strips, it was left to dry into a hard shell. Then came the second and third coats of the same strips, letting them dry in between applications. Now you have a pretty thick shell that is ready for painting and the cutting of windows for the boys to hang their heads out of as the float passed down the streets in the parade. The giant shoe was one of mom's greatest masterpieces. All of the Cub Scouts had a great time building it and riding in it. David K. still talks about building and riding in that shoe when he was a Cub Scout. Mom made many other costumes as well. She made two papier-mâché elephant heads for my cousin Jimmy and me. They had trunks, big ears and eyes you could see out of. She covered them with a gray cloth fabric that made them look extremely real and then made costumes from the same material that had the elephant feet attached to them. We won first place at the hollowing parade. That was to be expected though, because her creations always won first place. She made a funnel-shaped clown that had a head on top of a pole that extended through the top of the funnel. When were inside of the funnel costume, you would raise the head up and down and spin it round and round. It was a real novelty. One of my personal favorites was the giant Humpty Dumpty. It had small cut out eyes that were perfect for my bean shooter. I would take a bag of navy beans and shoot them at the judges up on the stage from inside of the Humpty Dumpty costume. I had to be sneaky about it so the judges could not figure out where the beans were coming from. As I sit here writing this, I can't help but wonder where all those fabulous creative costumes ever disappeared to. I can still visualize them in my memories so I guess I will always have them when I want to see them. It's good to have a photographic memory.

MORTGAGES

One evening I was at the laundromat and I overheard two women talking. One woman was telling the other that she was going to the bank in the morning to refinance her house mortgage because the mortgage rates were down to 5%. The next day I went to the bank and refinanced my mortgages that were currently at a rate of 7.25%. The bank asked me if I wanted lower payments or time deducted from the mortgages? I had the payments lowered this time. When I bought my farm, I bought it in two stages. First, I bought the land and had a mortgage on it. Second, I took out a construction loan to build my house with, which had a time limit of three months to complete and then I had to start paying a mortgage on the house. I got paid every two weeks, so I would pay one mortgage or the other each payday. This worked out very well because I would be a payment ahead on one mortgage when the spring property taxes came due, and I would skip that payment and use that money to pay the spring property taxes with. When the fall property taxes came due, I would be a month ahead on the other mortgage and I would pay the taxes with that money instead of making a mortgage payment, which put me back on track. When the interest rates would drop a little more, I would refinance my mortgages again, but this time, I had them deduct time off my mortgages so they would be paid off sooner! The payments had been reduced enough that I could go ahead and pay the money that I saved from lowering the interest rates, on the principle which also reduced the amount of money I was paying interest on! The bank asked me if I wanted to consolidate my two mortgages into one mortgage and just have one payment each month. I told them, "Hell no!" When I explained my system of payments, they said that they understood and wouldn't change it either! At the beginning of this story, I was wrapped up in an ongoing divorce. At the hearing, the judge was shocked to hear that I was building a house! He said, "Who would build a house in the middle of a divorce!" I said, "I would, because I'm tired of living in my car!" I was glad that I had a good relationship with the people at the bank and they knew I would always make things right with them. That's the advantage of doing business with a small-town bank. I think a big city bank would have pushed me out the door!

MOVING A HOUSE

O n the Ohio River the common pool stage is around 27 feet. Flood stage is 52 feet which has the river waters lapping at the edge of Highway 56 as it winds along the river through Aurora, Indiana. When I was a teenager, the state highway commission wanted to raise the level of the road high enough so the river would not flood the highway. When the road is under water, it is not usable and has to be closed. In order to elevate the roadway, the highway commission had to purchase all of the houses along the route and demolition them. One of the programs the highway commission instituted was to sell the houses to someone who was willing to tear it down or move it for only a few dollars. Most of these houses were in really good shape. Some of the houses were torn down for the materials to be used elsewhere. Some of the more industrious buyers bought them to move elsewhere. One of the most spectacular moves was made overnight. The buyer had previously prepared the house for moving by jacking it up and placing timbers beneath the house with wheeled fixtures beneath the timbers for rolling it down the highway. It was a large two-story house with a porch on it.

Phone and electric wires had to be lifted or removed so the house could travel down the street, meeting no resistance. A large barge was tied at the ferry landing about a mile up the road from the house. Thousands of pieces of wooden boards and timbers were woven and stacked together to make a large ramp to the barge. All kinds of lights were set in place to light up the work area at the barge. Hundreds of townspeople gathered at the landing to watch as the house came slowly up the street being pulled by a semi truck. It took most of the night to move the huge house from its former foundation to the ferry landing and up the ramp and onto the barge. The sun was coming up as the workers loaded all the ramp materials onto the barge for use again when unloading the house. The house's final destination was Warsaw, Kentucky. I never knew exactly where it finally came to rest, but it sure made a very interesting houseboat while it was on that barge!

MOVING

A local man in our town was moving into an apartment in another town 5 miles away. He was not married and had lived with his mother in their family home until she passed on. He had no vehicle and needed help in moving all of his possessions. One of our scout leaders had a large box truck and volunteered our Boy Scout troop to help the man move. The truck and the troop of Boy Scouts met at the man's house one Saturday morning to load up everything. Everything, was an understatement! It was going to take 3 to 4 full truckloads to hopefully move it all. He had been collecting things all of his life. He had already moved his furniture somehow and that was a big help to us. He had rented three storage garages and we filled them totally full. It is hard to imagine how someone could collect that much stuff and have it crammed into a small home. We must have thrown a construction dumpster full of just plain junk away. Why do people save worthless items in bulk like that? I accumulate a lot of things myself, but everything I collect is useful in some regard. I have three garages full of stuff, but they are large things like shelving and school type lockers along the walls with bigger things such as lawnmowers, trailers, tools and a farm tractor. It doesn't take much of those kinds of things to fill a garage. There are items on the shelves and in the lockers which help cut down on the clutter and keep things organized. Even then, I think to myself, I would sure hate to have to move. I know it would take me forever to move all the things I have collected throughout my lifetime. In another garage I have school lockers also plus woodworking tools, such as a full-size drill press, table saw, belt sander, radial arm saw and a full-size workbench. I also have butchering equipment and a large four-door commercial reach in box refrigerator. My motorcycle is also there, but my Civil War cannon takes up a pretty good amount of space also. My third garage is my largest garage. I rented my house there and I granted the tenants, use of that garage, which is still half-full of my equipment. I have run out of space to store things! My house in the city is on a main thoroughfare where there is a lot of traffic and it is a good place to have yard sales. I have reduced my inventory of things that I do not need or have several of, by having a yard sale occasionally on a Saturday. I am not the young man that I used to be and I try to avoid moving a lot of things around, especially the heavy items. I really miss that young man and I wonder where he went, meaning myself. Life is like a roll of toilet paper, the closer to the end you get, the faster it goes!

MR. PEEPERS

M y wife and I like to go to the cinemas on the weekends. We don't always attend the same cinema each time, we go to various ones depending on what movies are showing. After parking the car one evening, we were walking through the parking lot toward the front doors to the cinema, when I heard a peep peep peeping sound coming from a lone goose chick which is called a gosling. It was running all around calling for its mother which it was obviously separated from. I looked all around but I could see no Mother Goose or any more gosling's. I thought to myself, I'm sure this gosling has never been to the movies. I was wearing a hooded sweatshirt with pockets. So I went over to the little gosling and picked him up gently and put him in my pocket. I called him Mr. Peepers and he nestled down very comfortably in my pocket without making a sound. We went into the cinema and watch the movie. When we came out I drove down to the end of the parking lot where they have a small lake and a fountain. I thought maybe we might find some other geese there where I could leave Mr. Peepers with some of his relatives. But alas, there were no other geese to be found. Mr. Peepers got to take his first ride in an automobile as we traveled home to my house. I gave him some water and feed and he settled down for the night. The next day was Monday which is Boy Scout meeting night. We took Mr. Peepers to the meeting to meet the boys. I am always bringing something to the meetings to show the boys and give them a little hands-on experience and learning. All a person had to do was pat his hand on the ground and Mr. Peepers would come running to them. He was the highlight of the evening. All of the scouts and the adults alike got a chance to hold him and pet him. He made no bones about it he seemed to love it and was very open to associating with people. I sent Mr. Peepers home with one of the adult leaders who had a farm with a pond and some geese on it. The little gosling needed to be in his own environment with his own kind. I am not one to deprive him of it. I bid the little fellow goodbye as he left to be in a world of his own. Good luck to you Mr. Peepers!

MR. SHELBY

My Industrial Arts teacher at Aurora High School was Mr. Robert Shelby. He was a very learned man and taught me most everything I know about running a machine shop and using the equipment in it. But, I would have to say that he is most remembered for using a paddle and giving swats to various students that he deemed, worthy of punishment. If a student received 25 or more swats in a year's time period, he was allowed the honor, of signing, Mr. Shelby's paddle. If you were talking in his class and everything became quiet all of a sudden, you knew someone was going to get a swat and that someone he saw talking, was probably yourself! You would get this feeling as if someone punched you in the stomach, when you looked to see Mr. Shelby pointing at you and saying," Come up, brother Block!" You knew you were in trouble now and you are going to receive Mr. Shelby's wrath. When you came to the front of the room, he would tell the unlucky person to assume the position, which was bent over, grabbing the edges of his desk. He reminded me of a golfer with his upswing stroke. Often, the person's feet would lift from the floor, while receiving the swat. Teachers, today, would not dare to touch a student in any manner. Today's students are so unruly and take advantage of this fact. Students would be more behaved and have more respect for their teachers, if physical punishment was practiced in the form of swats from a paddle! I took my share of the swats when I was in school and I told my children's teachers to let them have the same, if they deserved it, because they would have my support and my permission to do so. But, in today's society, punishment is left up to the parents. Manners and respect is something to be learned at home and taken to school, not the other way around. If Mr. Shelby was here today, delivering the same punishment, he would probably be in jail or in court more often than in school! We need those long-gone teachers and rules in our schools today! Our school systems would be more productive and graduate a better class of students. Mr. Shelby was a great teacher and took no crap!

MY BIRTHDAY

My birthday is coming up in a few days and my wife asked me what I would like for my birthday? I have gotten to the age of where I don't like to have birthdays because they make me feel old. Face it, I am old! I thought for a minute and then I told her that I would like to win the lottery for my birthday or maybe have a younger body, with no aches and pains or maybe just be alone and have some peace and quiet for myself, without a bunch of people fussing over me. But of course, these are all things that are impossible to have. With that in mind, I told her all I want is for her to be happy. I know that would make me happy!

MY PITCH

Keep in mind Forrest Gump and Huckleberry Finn. My name is Richard Block and I have written a book titled, Life as I Lived it, Small town country living. I referred to Forrest and Huckleberry, because my book centers around a small town on the bank of the Ohio River in Indiana from the 1950s to present day, following the adventures of a youth growing up there. This is a book compiled of 122 true short stories of a way of life, long gone into the past. Memories of a reader's childhood come to life as they read this book. Combining all the stories creates an autobiography of a very versatile and adventurous boy, which is me, experiences growing up in many situations that are humorous, historical and educational, which will put a new twist on any similar movie or sitcom. All of the stories combined blend into one autobiographical story. Separately, each story can be an episode of a sitcom.

NEIGHBORS

In my small-town neighborhood where I grew up, I knew almost everyone who lived on my street and they knew me. Most of my neighbors were elderly retired people. There were lots of occupations that these people knew very well and if you were willing to learn, they would teach you what they knew. I learned a lot from my neighbors as I grew up. I was always willing to learn from the different tradesmen that lived in my neighborhood. I learned all kinds of carpentry and concrete work. I learned how to build stone walls, lay brick and block and how to mix concrete from scratch. There was always a neighbor willing to give a hand in any project I was wrapped up in. After I grew up and moved away to different places, I discovered that neighbors in new locations were greatly different. Some neighbors were very friendly while other neighbors did not care to know me at all. Here in the big city I only know one or two of my neighbors and that is all. I have never met my neighbor next door to me who has lived there several years. The neighbors here are not as close or as friendly as other places I have lived. At my farm in Milan, Indiana, I know all my neighbors. Whenever I need something, there is always someone there to help and when they need something, I am happy to return the favor. We go places and do things together frequently. It is great to have neighbors that care and watch out for each other. I miss that when I am in the big city. Sometimes I wonder if I were to be hit by a car and was lying in the street, would any of them take the time to drag my body out of the way! Sometimes you will find it's the people you least expect to do something for you, that help you the most, in an emergency situation.

PARTY LINES

It always seemed that we were behind the times in the small river town of Aurora, Indiana. Our phone system consisted of real phone operators that worked in the phone exchange. When you wanted to call someone, you picked up your phone and the operator would say," Number please" and you would tell the phone operator the phone number of the person you wanted to call. We did not get the dial system until 1966. That was an easy date for me to remember because that is when I graduated high school. One of the good things about the old system when you had operators is that if you really needed to contact someone right away and their phone line was busy, you could have the operator break in on their conversation and tell them someone was needing to contact them immediately. Sometimes the operator would simply plug you in to their busy phone conversation and you would have three people on the same line all at one time. Sometimes you would get plugged in on a busy line without the people knowing it and you simply listened to them talk. They would be totally unaware you were listening in unless you spoke up and said something! I guess you could determine that as what we now call a conference call which is something that did not exist at that time. If you had a private line you had a four digit phone number and had the line all to yourself. If you were on a party line, you could have as many as four people sharing the same phone number with the exception of the letter on the end of the phone number. For example, my old phone number was 136M and the lady down the street was 136W and the lady up the street was 136R. The 136J was not assigned to anyone at that time. The letters, M, W, R and J were the letters that were always used behind the three-digit prefix. The two ladies on our party line could simply pick up their phones at the same time and just talk without going through the operator. This they would do every day at 6:00 PM and talk for an hour or two. This was very aggravating if we wanted to use our phone to call someone. If you asked them to hang up, they would think you to be rude and just keep talking. If you told them it was an emergency, they would usually let you have the line to make your call. I liked to aggravate them when they were tying up the line. I would go outside to the phone fuse box where the telephone lines came into the house and take a screwdriver and rake it across the terminals causing an ear shattering static, then, I would put my screwdriver across the terminals and short out the line so it could not be used. One of them would go to their neighbor's house and use their phone to call the phone company repair man. I would watch for the repair man to arrive in his truck and walk up to the front door of the lady's house. As soon as he went inside, I took the screwdriver out so the line would be working fine. After doing this for so many times the repair man refused to come because he knew there was nothing wrong with the line every time he showed up! I know that sounds mean, but they were always tying up the phone line. Pansy was the name of the lady that lived down the street across from my house. Later on, in years after most of her relatives had passed on she called me one day and asked me to come over to her house. I was surprised. I could not imagine what she wanted from me. It turned out that she had a light burnt out in her kitchen and had no one to help her replace it. I felt sorry for her and fixed her light. I told her any time she needed help to just call me and I would be there for her. I think at that point we finally became friends. If you lived in the country, you had the old-fashioned wall phones that were wooden and had a crank on the side to ring the operator. You also had party lines and when you were called, your phone would ring long and short rings to determine which person the phone call was intended for. You got very used to listening to the phone every time it rang and counted the long and short rings to determine if the phone call was for you or someone else on the party line. What a difference the dial system made! It was interesting if you were away from home in a large city and you wanted to make a call back home. You had to go through the operator and tell her your phone number and she would put it through manually. It was comical sometimes if the operator was not familiar with the old phone system because they would be baffled at how to handle the call. Most of the time you had to explain to them that you did not have a modern dial system such as they have been using for many years. As a kid, you got used to teaching an operator how to put a call through to reach the old system phone number even though she was an adult. Brings back memories for some of us old folks, doesn't it?

PERFECTION

I have always been a perfectionist. I try to be perfect in everything I do. My scoutmaster used to call me the neat one, because I always kept my things so neatly kept in order. I hate to have to do things over and over. Most of the time, I overdo things, because once I fix something, I want it to stay fixed, permanently! I strive to always do things right the first time and to always be right when I make a statement. It makes my wife mad sometimes, because she's always asking me if I always have to be right? I just tell her, I try to be right, as often as I can be. But of course, it doesn't always work out that way. I thought I was wrong once, but I was mistaken! That's a joke, of course, because no matter how hard I try, I can't always be right or perfect, no matter how hard I strive to be. I am sure there are a lot of people who strive to do the same. My mother said that I was the only perfect person she ever knew. She said I was a perfect idiot! I was always proud that I was perfect at something! My mother had a great sense of humor!

PRIVATE JET TRAVEL

There are companies that have private jets for hire. You simply drop $100,000 in an account for them to draw from and you can have a private jet and crew at your disposal, any time you want it and it will take you anywhere you want to go. You can also request meals or snacks to be served on board during the flight. A friend of mine frequently used this service to travel to his various properties in Michigan and Florida, leaving from the Lunken Airport in Cincinnati. Traveling by private jet is so simple and easy. You drive your car out to where the plane is waiting on the runway, climb on board while your luggage is being stored away and take off! There is no red tape, no security and no waiting for anything. You just get on the plane and leave while an attendant parks your car. I asked the pilot if there is any problem with passengers carrying firearms. He said there were no restrictions or any problems with it and to carry anything I like. I told him I like to carry at least two handguns on me when I travel and he said that was perfectly fine. My friend Lou had an English bulldog named George that he would take with him on flights to his properties. Private jets are designed like a living room with plush chairs that have no seatbelts. Some chairs face forward and others face rearward so people can sit and talk to each other face-to-face. I remember one flight when Lou placed George on a rearward facing seat and Lou sat opposite of him, facing forward. We taxied out onto the runway and when we were cleared for takeoff, the pilot shoved the throttle forward and we took off like a bullet! George went flying from his seat and slid down the aisle a on his stomach like a sack of potatoes! Lou almost had a heart attack and I almost died laughing! Once we were in the air everything became normal. It was so nice when the plane landed, because a car would drive out to the plane and load us and our luggage up and take us to our destination with no hassles, red tape or security problems. I always enjoyed that way of traveling but, it is very expensive!

PROFESSIONAL ATHLETES

The amount of monies paid to professional athletes is overwhelming most of the time. Typically, when a person such as an athlete makes a large amount of money, he lives it up, spending it like there is no end to it. In a short length of time when he no longer makes that large amount of money anymore due to age or injury, he finds that he has spent most all of it and still has large debts to pay. The lifespan of a football player is 4 or 5 years on the field if he's lucky. After that, he is washed up and out of the game. It's the same way in any sports. There are players however, that do not live for the moment, but save or invest their money wisely while they still have it. A good friend of mine had a grandson who played basketball in college and was first pick on the draft list after graduation. He was picked by team and played professional basketball. He wasn't the star of the team but he made a good salary. He was smart with his money and put it into savings and allowed himself an allowance to live on instead of living it up and spending it like other players do. He played basketball for several years for several teams. He continued to save his money and spend it wisely when it was needed. When he eventually left the game of basketball behind, he took his savings and went into business with his brother buying and rehabbing condominiums and other pieces of property which is what he is still doing to this very day. You have to plan for the future. You will find that you can't always be on top of the world no matter how you make your living or how much money you make. It's unavoidable. It's called old age and common sense.

PULL TAB

Every Thanksgiving we usually have a get together at our house and have a big Thanksgiving meal with all the trimmings. Besides all the camaraderie and good time storytelling about everyone's children and grandchildren, there is the cleanup and the putting away of the leftovers. All of the ladies are excited because the day after Thanksgiving is Black Friday. Black Friday is one of the major shopping holidays of the year for the department stores. Everyone is out doing their Christmas shopping and there is a mad rush to cash in on the bargains the stores have to offer. I always save the pull tabs from the soda pop and beer cans for my granddaughter who takes them to school, where they are collected from all the students and donated to the Ronald McDonald House's fundraiser. The pull tabs are relatively pure aluminum and are sold to scrap yards, where they bring a very nice price, to support the Ronald McDonald House. While the ladies were cleaning up the turkey dinner leftovers and putting them in the refrigerator, I was attempting to put a pull tab in my collection jar on the counter next to the refrigerator, when I noticed my niece, Sandy, was bent over revealing her butt crack! I thought to myself, gee, here's a rare opportunity to place the pull tab into the slot she created! So, I dropped the pull tab into the butt crack slot with only one person noticing but kept it secret. Later on, in the wea hours of Black Friday morning, Sandy had this strange feeling that something wasn't just right! The other ladies had shared the secret among themselves about the pull tab in Sandy's pants. They began laughing and asking Sandy what was wrong? She said she didn't know but she felt uncomfortable and started dancing all around in the department store that they were shopping in. It looked like a version of the Teaberry shuffle! One of the ladies told her that I had dropped a pull tab down her pants while she was putting something into the refrigerator. Sandy went behind a clothes rack to try and get it out, but there were too many shoppers and she was in the middle of a crowd! She finally went out to her car in the parking lot where she could make a thorough search for the pull tab. To make a long story short, she saved the pull tab, gift wrapped it and gave it to me for Christmas! What a unique gift!

RONALD MCDONALD HOUSE

W hat year this was I do not remember, but in 1974 the first Ronald McDonald House was opened in Philadelphia, Pennsylvania. It was a new concept provided by McDonald's restaurants to provide a home away from home for families who had a child in a local hospital for treatment. It was an interesting concept and it was operated much in the same way as a fraternity or sorority house. The house had a live-in manager who oversaw all everything that went on there. Each family had their own individual room, which was all their own, to be cleaned and maintained by the family occupying it. A community kitchen was provided with multiple cook stoves and refrigerators which were shared by all the families staying there. Each family would label whatever items they stored in the cabinets or refrigerators in the kitchen. I thought it was a great program and I thought we had a great need for a Ronald McDonald House here in Cincinnati. I approached my boss, Mr. Groen about the possibility of having one here. He did not seem to be very supportive of the project. Finally, Mr. Groen was approached by some of the medical staff of Children's Hospital who were hoping to get Mr. Groen to support the institution of a

Ronald McDonald House near Children's Hospital here in Cincinnati. It was finally agreed that the best way to resolve the undertaking was to go and visit the nearest Ronald McDonald House which happened to be in Chicago, Illinois. It was early December when Mr. Groen, his lawyer and some of his staff boarded his private motor coach, driven by myself and headed for Chicago. When we arrived at the Ronald McDonald House, there was a man chipping ice and shoveling snow from the walks and steps leading into the house. We later found out that the man was one of the family members staying there. The house manager told us that the residents there all pitch in at times to help with the chores. The house itself was two or three stories tall and very clean and very neat as well as very organized. Mr. Groen and everyone involved were very impressed. In the years to come a Cincinnati Ronald McDonald House was constructed near the Children's Hospital. It was a two-story, very modern and very beautiful house with all the amenities of all the other Ronald McDonald houses, including a very professional house manager. With the support of Mr. Groen's 42 McDonald's restaurants around the greater Cincinnati area, the original Ronald McDonald house eventually fell by the wayside to a bigger and better house that was 10 times the size of the old one and still in a location that was within walking distance of the Children's Hospital. The last time I visited the Ronald McDonald House, I was in awe of the advancements that had been made in the Ronald McDonald House Organization. What a wonderful place McDonald's has provided for families of children in need from all over the world to come here with their child to be treated at nearby hospitals. Thank you, McDonald's, and everyone concerned.

RUNAWAY JEEP

We were in Pennsylvania, headed for the East Coast, on a fall, sightseeing trip. I was driving my boss and his wife, plus a couple of guests, in his 40 foot long, MCI motor coach, with his Jeep Wagoneer, being towed behind. My boss, Lou, liked to travel to Vermont and Maine to watch the leaves turn color in the fall season. I was driving down a long hill and I could see some construction ahead with a long line of orange barrels that closed the right lane and moved the traffic to the lane on the left. As I approached the long line of barrels, I put on my left turn signal and checked my mirrors for traffic, getting ready to move over to the left lane, when I noticed some idiot in a Jeep, trying to pass me on the right shoulder of the highway! I looked at my TV monitor, which had a camera mounted on the rear of the bus, to watch behind the bus, when I was backing up or towing a vehicle and I noticed the Jeep was gone! I looked at the right mirror again, only to notice that it was our Jeep which had broken loose and was in the process of passing us on the right-hand side of the bus! The construction barrels were coming up fast and I had to react at once! I quickly sped up and moved over in front of the Jeep with the bus. I slowed down ever so carefully and let the Jeep come up to my rear bumper very gently. I slowly applied the brakes and brought us to a stop just in front of the first barrel. Everyone onboard, breathed a sigh of relief as I stepped out to inspect the Jeep. The Jeep was fine and there was no damage to the bus or the Jeep, but now, someone was going to have to drive the Jeep to where we were going to spend the night. Lou volunteered and did a good job getting the Jeep to where it had to go for the night. Early the next morning, I took the Jeep to the closest gas station, to fill it up and get some information on where I could get some repairs made to the tow bar. Another customer at the filling station told me of a place, but he could not tell me how to get there. He said he was going in that direction and I could follow him there, which, I did. Once I was there, I understood why he couldn't tell me how to get there. The repair shop was in an old barn on a back road. The shop owner was very primitive and is only tools were an anvil, a cutting torch and a welder. The ears of the brackets on the bumper had sheared off and the tow bar was twisted. I was feeling a little skeptical, that this man would be able to fix everything, back to where it was usable. To my surprise, the man was amazing! As I looked around his shop, I noticed he had repaired some gears from farm machinery by welding and forming new teeth on them. As I watched, he cut new pieces from a sheet of steel that fit perfectly with his torch. He drilled them and welded them into place, which repaired the bumper brackets. Then heated the twisted arm of the tow bar and hammered it back into place on his anvil. I thought to myself, it will be a miracle if it fits into place on the bumper! Again, to my surprise, it fit perfectly as he put the pins into place that held the tow bar to the bumper! Wow! I couldn't believe it! " How much do I owe you for this," I asked. When he told me, 35 bucks, I couldn't believe that either! That's country folks for you.

RUNNING THE TRAP LINE

As a youth, I learned many things from my uncle Leonard and one of the main things I learned was how to set traps and catch animals. I bought many of my steel traps from a distant relative, named Art Conaway, who consistently attended auctions and flea markets, where he maintained a constant supply of used steel traps. My grandmother was a person who was always visiting the relatives and that is how I came to know my cousin Art. I had a wooden, 10-foot, V bow boat, that I traded five, young, frying size groundhogs, to my uncle for, with a small outboard motor, which I used to locate muskrat dens on North Hogan Creek. I wore hip boots and walked along the creek bank in the water, to find the best places, to set my traps. I kept my boat close to me, so if I would happen to step into a deep place, I could dive onto the front deck of the boat, instead of getting a bath in the icy cold November water. The Indiana trapping season always started on November 15th each year, which gave me about three weeks of good trapping weather before the creeks freeze over. I learned to keep an eye on the water level of the Ohio River and the creeks, because if the water level would raise, the traps would be too deep to catch anything. On the other hand, if the water level dropped, the traps would be exposed, and the animals would avoid them. Occasionally I would catch a raccoon, but I was mainly after muskrats and mink. I would get up early, every morning on school days and check my traps on foot from the creek bank, before going to school. I always carried a burlap bag, also known as a gunnysack, to put my spare traps and muskrats in. Most of the time, the weight of the trap would drown the muskrat, but occasionally I would have one alive, waiting for me. A wrap on the head with a traps stake, would take care of business in short order. My neighbors were old Kentuckians, and I would give them the muskrat meat for their supper meal. They were always glad to get it fresh. I remember there were times when my hands were so frozen from handling traps and animals in the water, that I had a difficult time, trying to turn the doorknob, to get into the house! I had a dozen stretchers of different sizes, to stretch hides on, after skinning, so they could dry out and the excess fat removed from the hide. When the trapping season ended, my uncle and I would get together and sell our furs. Fur prices would vary every year and we would shop around for the fur buyer, giving the best prices and sell our furs to him. I had a bank account at the People's Building and Loan, where I always put my money and left it there, to use when I might need it. I remember, I bought my first Ruger .22 rifle in 1964 with some of that money and I still have it today! I think how expensive the $55 was back then! Now, that same rifle costs over $200 more! Inflation, how will we ever contend with it?

SAILING SHIPS OF OLD

D id you ever wonder how the old-time sailing ships with their tall masts and huge sails kept from falling over and lying on their sides? Well, this was accomplished with the use of ballast stones. Ballast stones are a smooth brick-shaped stone about the size of a concrete block. These were put in the bottom of the ship as a counterweight when it was not carrying cargo. As a ship was loaded with cargo an equal weight of ballast stones would be removed and left on the dock to be reused by other ships when needed. One of the most dangerous cargos that these ships would transport was manure. This manure was an important fertilizer for the farmers in the colonies. Insurance companies of that time period were very hesitant about insuring ships carrying a cargo of manure because the manure would occasionally get wet or extremely damp and when this happened, the manure cargo produced a form of methane gas. If this happened and a crewman went below deck with a lighted lantern or candle, the gas would ignite, and the ship would blow up and burn. In order to keep this from happening there was a practice formulated to keep the manure dry as possible during shipment. This practice was known as Ship High In Transit. By not putting the cargo in the very bottom of the ship, but storing it high during transportation, made it much safer for everyone concerned. This way the cargo was less likely to get wet and not be in a damp environment inside the ship. The abbreviation for Ship High in Transit is S.H.I.T. That is how manure came to be a word of its own. It has been construed to be a naughty word but it is merely the first letters of a shipping term. And that is how manure got to be known by the four-letter word. When a ship was short on crewmembers, a team of sailor's web search out the bars along the docks for prospective crewmembers. When a ship is sailing in the ocean it leans to one side because the wind is pushing it along in that direction. The tables where the crew ate their meals were mounted to one side of the ship's hull and the other end of the table was suspended from the rafter above by a piece of rope and a pulley. In this manner the table could be adjusted to a more level position while the ship was leaning to one side as it sailed. Crewman were in the habit of putting their elbows on the table and bracketing their cups and plates to keep them from sliding back and forth on the table as the ship rocked back and forth with the waves. The team of sailors who are out to Shanghai prospective crewmembers would look for patrons in the bar who were putting their elbows on the tables as they ate. This was a sure sign that this person had been to sea previously and was a good prospect. This is why your mommy and daddy always told you not to put your elbows on the table without really knowing why they were telling you this! They just thought it was bad manners because they were always told the same! Now you have learned a little about ships of long ago.

SAW MUSIC

My duties at McDonald's as a supervisor, was to take care of everything from the rooftop to the blacktop. As a result of these duties, I had accounts at many hardware stores. The reason for the many accounts was their locations in relation to the closest McDonald's restaurant. There was a hardware store in Clifton on McMillan Street that I used frequently, because there were three McDonald's located in that vicinity. I became well acquainted with Tom, the store owner. We struck up a conversation one day, when I came in to buy a hand saw. He told me about a man who played the saw. I asked what he meant by playing the saw? He said this man would come into his store every time a new shipment of saws arrived and play various ones to see how they sounded. If he found one, he liked, he would buy it. He would sit on a chair with the saw handle on his knee and held the tip of the saw with his left, gloved hand. He would then bow the saw slightly and with a violin bow, he would play the saw on the non-toothed edge, like a violin. Tom said the man would give a regular concert, playing all kinds of tunes as he tried out each saw. I never got to hear the man play, but I knew exactly what the technique was. Sometimes, I would see it done on country-western musical shows on TV. Many years later, my wife and I were in a bar on Abaco Island, in the Bahamas, with some friends, when we encountered a young boy that my friends knew and struck up a conversation with him. My friend Carl asked the young man what he was doing nowadays, and he told Carl that he was in a band. I asked him what musical instrument he played, and he said the saw! He told us where he was playing that evening and invited us to come and see him and the band perform. I thought that was amazing that he was going to play a saw! When we arrived, the band was already playing. When I saw the young man doing his thing, playing the saw took on a whole new meaning! He was holding the saw by the handle and raking a screwdriver up and down the saw's teeth, making a sandpaper like, rhythmic sound! It sounded really good, even though I thought he was hilarious!

SKIL BOAR GUN

C lyde Crosby was the other half of our maintenance department at McDonalds of Cincinnati. I was the other half and we took care of any repairs from the rooftop to the blacktop for the 42 McDonalds restaurants in the Greater Cincinnati area market. We were constantly using drills and stringing extension cords everywhere we worked. One day Clyde bought a cordless battery-operated drill and tested using it on the job. It did okay at times but was not very powerful and the battery did not last long enough to suit me. You had to plug the whole drill in over night to charge it up and it always seem to go dead when you were in the middle of something, which was typical of those early model drills. I held off buying one in hopes that someday a better battery-operated drill would hit the market. One day I walked into One of the electrical supply houses to get some supplies and there was a factory rep from the Skil Company demonstrating their latest battery-operated drill. It was the answer to my dreams. It featured a removable battery pack that would quick charge in one hour and had 2 speeds, one for drilling and a lower speed for driving screws. With an extra battery pack, it didn't matter about the charging time, you were always ready to keep on going by switching batteries. I was impressed with the torque the drill had when it drove in a screw. I took the drill from the salesman's hand and said "I'll take it!" He said that I couldn't do that because it was his only demo model. I said to put it on my bill and order me another one as soon as possible. As I walked out the door with the drill, I heard him say he guessed that he was packing up, the demo was over, his drill has left the building! As soon as the shipment of the new drills arrived, I picked up another one plus extra batteries and holsters that were made specifically for the new Boar guns. The first time I walked on the job site with those drills in their holsters on my belt, the other construction workers taunted me about being Wyatt Earp and laughing at me. I had a drill bit in one drill and a screwdriver bit in the other. The taunting and laughter soon stopped and turned into amazement and wonder when I pulled those boar guns from their holsters and used them. I would drill a hole with one and drive a screw with the other, drill a hole, drive a screw, drill a hole, drive a screw, just like a one – two punch in a fight! Who's the funny guy now!, I thought to myself. I was knocking out work in a third of the time it normally took. I must of made a big impression on the construction workers, because the next McDonalds that was being built had everyone using them! Those Boar Guns served me well for a number of years. Since that time, bigger, better and a lot more powerful drills have flooded the market. The Skil Boar Guns are just a piece of history now, but they were great in their day!

SNORKELING

As a kid, I always had a fear of water because of a drowning experience I had. It took me a long time to get over it and I did not learn how to swim until I was about 15 or 16 years old. I knew I had to learn how to swim or I would never reach the rank of Eagle Scout. My fellow scout and close friend, Marty Henry was instrumental in helping me learn how to swim. I always thought Marty was part fish. He was as much at home in the water as he was on land. He could swim like a fish and dive to the bottom of the lake and retrieve items accidentally dropped from the dock. Swimming in freshwater is quite different than swimming in salt water. I found that a person is more buoyant in salt water than in freshwater. When I was in the Caribbean, I went on several snorkeling excursions offshore from several islands and in different locations. The water was always so clear and you could dive down and pick up things from the ocean floor. After a period of time, I bought my own snorkeling equipment. I like the better equipment with the purge valves so one can ballast out any water that seeps into the mask or the snorkel. I have dry snorkels. They have a valve at the end of the tip that closes automatically when water tries to seep into the snorkel tube. There is nothing more distasteful than a mouth full of saltwater! I found that I could relax so much while snorkeling that I could just about go to sleep. Most small boat captains make the people that are going to snorkel, wear a floatation vest for their own safety. You really don't need one in salt water because you are so buoyant and they make it a little more difficult to dive down to the bottom to get seashells and such. Some of my best souvenirs are shells that I retrieved from the bottom of the ocean. I liked snorkeling so well that I became an instructor for snorkeling in the Boy Scouts. It is a great sport; I think everyone should try it at least once!

SOCIAL SECURITY

The goal of most every American is to get a good education and find a good job that pays well enough for him to afford owning a home and raising a family. With every paycheck, you are paying all kinds of taxes. Percentages of your paycheck go to Federal Income tax, State Income tax, Social Security tax, city tax, sales tax, and gasoline tax, every time you buy gasoline. The gasoline tax is added into the price of the gasoline and is there to help maintain our highways. Then you have loans to pay and the interest that goes with them. Let's not forget property taxes twice a year! It just seems like I could go on and on about taxes. You try to set money aside for retirement in 401(k)s and pension funds. This money is taken automatically from your check and you don't really see it. There are lots of people who do not have retirement funds or other incomes from investments and try to live on Social Security alone. Once you have your house paid for and retire, you find you can't afford to live in your own home with the cost of monthly bills eating up your Social Security check each month. Besides the monthly bills, you do not realize how much money you used to spend eating in restaurants and putting gasoline in your car, until you retire. The really unfair practice levied by the government on you, is that you are required by law, to pay income tax on the relatively poor amount of money you receive from Social Security! How many times do you have to pay tax on the same money! This needs to be changed! Our government is ripping us off! For what little money you received from Social Security at the end of the month, you should not have to pay any income tax at the end of the year, is the way I feel about it. Social Security hardly pays enough to live on and then the government wants 25% of it back! What's wrong with this picture people!

SPEEDING TICKET

I was working for a company that sold security systems in the mid to 2000's and I had to go to the courthouse in Lafayette, Indiana to make a minor repair to their security system. We were having trouble communicating with their system online because of one of the connections at their courthouse. I was returning to Cincinnati on I-74, when I noticed the State Trooper's police car behind me with his lights flashing. I knew I had been driving 90 to 100 miles an hour, but I had been trying to slow down whenever I noticed how fast I was going. After we were safely parked alongside the interstate, the trooper walked up to my window, which I had rolled down and asked for my driver's license and registration. He asked me if I knew how fast I was going? I, of course told him, "I really wasn't sure." He then told me that he clocked me at 85 mph. I said, "You've got to be kidding!" "I thought I was going slow to the point of feeling almost stopped!" I, then told him that I had just gotten back from Germany a week ago and was accustomed to driving 130 mph on the autobahn. That's why I felt I was going pretty slow. I figured he was going to give me a ticket no matter what I said, so I told him, "You should've seen how fast I was going before I slowed down to where you clocked me at only 85 mph! He said," Well, I'm going to have to give you a ticket." I said, "Well, do your best!" He might have let me go if I had told him what job I was doing previously in the day. Do you ever have one of those days when you just don't give a crap!

STARTING FROM SCRATCH

When I first bought my farm, the property was in poor condition. A man who did logging had owned the property and had cut all the trees that were worth anything and then dropped the property into the bank's lap. The fields had been untouched on the 25-acre lower end and saplings 10 foot high were growing in abundance everywhere. These were fields that should have been farmed! The top 15-acre field near the county road was in poor condition, because the person farming that field had not been adding the fertilizers and nutrients the land needed to keep producing good crops. The roads were deeply rutted from erosion and off-road vehicles driving on them. There were junk cars, engine parts, pop machines, laundry machines and a dump, full of everyday trash and junk. The small house was a wreck with all kinds of graffiti painted on it. The roof leaked and the windows were broken out. The weather and rains took a toll on the interior of the house, destroying the flooring and the interior walls. There were some outbuildings that were just as bad. It took months of hauling things away and burning things that were burnable. I hired a man by the name of George Smith, who did the excavating. He spent eight hours of bulldozing, just to make the roads usable. After that, he used gravel from the creek to gravel the roads that he just cleared. He said I had enough sand and gravel in my creek bed to gravel all the roads in Ripley County. I later learned that over a period of time, a lot of sand and gravel had been hauled from there by the previous owner. I bought a tractor and bush hog and began mowing down the saplings that were growing in the lower 25-acre field. It took me a whole week just to do that. I literally destroyed both pieces of equipment getting the task done! I took soil samples from the fields and sent them to Purdue University for analysis. They sent me back a report of what nutrients I would need and how much in volume to put on my fields to bring them up to snuff. I made a deal with a local farmer to share crop my property and get the fields into working condition again. There were areas where the government had a program to pay me not to grow crops, but to let the land be set aside for wildlife purposes. I would bush hog {cut} some of these areas into a checkerboard shaped grid to improve wildlife habitat. Rabbits and quail, as well as other things, like to live along the edge of open areas. By doing this, it makes lots of edges everywhere, thus increasing the habitat areas. This was only the beginning, as I prepared my life for living on a farm.

STILL HUNTING

I am 67 years old at this time and I am still hunting. But that is not the meaning of Still Hunting. Still Hunting is a type of hunting practice. I have always used the art of still hunting all of my life while squirrel hunting. Deer hunting is a different kind of hunting practice. Most deer hunters hunt from elevated platforms in trees, known as deer stands. Some states do not allow hunters to hunt from an elevated platform, so the hunters have to remain on the ground in ground blinds or foxholes. Lots of hunters build small portable shack type blinds that are set permanently in place. Some of the permanent ones can get pretty elaborate with windows, a chair and some type of heat, which makes it pretty cozy for cold weather deer hunting. My father always told me, in regard to squirrel hunting, that the more ground a hunter covers, the more game he is going to encounter and this is true in deer hunting also. In my younger days, I used to hunt deer in Michigan every year for many years. At that time, hunters using firearms, had to hunt from the ground and were not permitted to use tree stands. This was no problem for me, because I was used to hunting squirrels and slipping silently through the woods. Still Hunting is the art of silently slipping through the woods in search of game. The general rule to Still Hunting is to take a step and then take a look and do more looking than you do stepping! Most of the time when I am still hunting, the animals usually walk up on me while I am in the still mode, meaning, just standing there daydreaming. I do a lot of daydreaming while I am hunting because it causes my body to stand still like a statue, while my mind is somewhere else entirely! The longer you stand in one place, the greater the chances are that the animals perceive you to be harmless and accept you as part of the landscape! An old-timer once taught me how to extend my range of hearing by cupping my hands and putting them behind my ears, bending them forward just a little and then slowly turning my head to direct my hearing in different directions. I do this frequently to hear as far away as I can. If I am satisfied that there is no game within hearing range, I will move forward a good distance so I can listen to areas that are now coming into range beyond where I could hear before. I would say that I have collected more game that sneaked up on me than I have collected by sneaking up on them while Still Hunting. Animals that live around a farm are used to hearing the motors of farm implements, so they pay very little attention to me when I ride into the woods on my 4-wheeler, stop in a good hunting area, turn it off and just sit there on it. I don't do a lot of walking anymore. Rolling around on 4 wheels is much easier and less tiring! My 4-wheeler is my best hunting companion when it comes to deer hunting. I shoot them and it drags them. What a great team player!

SUNKEN BOAT

When I was a teenager, I had a wooden 10-foot, V bowed boat that I used every day in the winter, to run my trap lines on Hogan Creek, which connected to the Ohio River at the mouth. The trapping season in Indiana always started at noon on November 15th. My neighbor, John H., who was two years younger than myself wanted to try trapping muskrats and raccoons, to make some money for his self. John bought a few traps and his parents bought him a 10-foot aluminum John boat. When I first saw John's new boat, I thought there was something missing or strange about it. I told his parents that I thought there was something wrong with the boat, but I just couldn't put my finger on what the problem was. After a week or two had gone by, I finally realized that the boat had no floatation material beneath the seats. I told them that on a rough day on the creek, when the weather was kicking up the waves, John's boat could possibly sink. They assured me that the boat was unsinkable according to the salesman that sold it to them. I told them the salesman did not know what he was talking about and the boat will sink in rough weather and high waves regardless of what the salesman told them. Of course, I was just a kid, telling grown-ups what is what and they just ignored my warning. Big mistake! About a week or so later, John came home, soaking wet and freezing on a bad, November weather day. When his parents asked, "Why are you soaking wet?" John replied, "The weather was bad and the waves were so high and the boat sank to the bottom of the creek in only a few seconds. The icy water was freezing cold and I was lucky to be able to make it to the shore and pull myself out of the water!" Late November is not a good time to go swimming and I do not think he was wearing a life preserver at the time. A few days later, John's parents contacted a state police diver, who went down and tied a rope on the boat and pulled it from the creek. John's parents promptly sold the boat and his gear and that was the end of John's trapping venture. A while later, John's parents admitted to me that I was right, that boat was sinkable! I bet that hurt!

TAKING A TRIP

Whenever I know I'm going to take a trip somewhere, I start several days in advance, making up a list of things to take. I simply jot down things as I think of them. I made up a list for the Boy Scouts titled, Things to Take Camping. It took me about five years to perfect it. It is a list of things to pick and choose from depending upon the time of the year. There are items on the list to choose from in the winter and things to choose from in the summer. It is a very versatile list for new and old Boy Scouts so that something they will be needing, is not overlooked. It's a great list for a camping trip, but for other kinds of trips, there are other things you need to take that do not apply to camping. It seems like the older you get the more forgetful you become and that's why I start early compiling a list of things to take for each trip, dependent on my destination and time of year. One of the things I overlook most is my binoculars. I have several pairs of 10 x 50 binoculars that save me a lot of walking. They are a little bit large in size, but they bring things up close with a wide field of view. I usually change the narrow neck strap that comes with the binoculars, to a wider neck strap that makes them more comfortable to wear around your deck. Smaller binoculars, that you can put in your pocket, seem to take a toll on my eyes, making them tired or sore by the end of the day, depending on how often I am using them. Binoculars are great to take to concerts and plays also. It enables me to see things going on in the background that you don't normally notice. Another thing I forget often is my camera. There are times when I miss out on some really great photo opportunities because my camera was left behind. I like to take with me, the full medical kit that I assembled, so that I am prepared for just about any situation that might arise. I usually start assembling the things on my personal list, a day or two in advance of my departure. There are usually things that I think of while I am putting things together that I did not have on my list. That is why it's smart to start packing early and putting items in the vehicle you are going to use. I always tell my wife, "If it's not in the van, it didn't make the trip!" Things like a pillow and a blanket make a trip more comfortable, if you are traveling very far. I try to think of the people traveling with me and what their needs might be to make the trip more pleasant. Snacks that are not messy are a must for children. Water or soda pop bottles with screw-on caps will make spills less current or eliminates them altogether. A good material list is the rule, rather than the exception and don't forget your medications! Happy traveling!

THE COLONOSCOPY

I had never had a colonoscopy before. This was my first time and it was totally different from the second time I had one. I didn't realize the adventure I was in for! I went to the doctor's office where I undressed and put the gown on that opened in the rear. I had no special instructions. I did not have to drink the milky chalk substance that they do now before the procedure, and they did not put me to sleep. They had me lay on my side on a table and the nurse gave me an enema using two, small, milk carton type containers. She told me when I felt the urge, to go into the bathroom and expel the liquid results. The nurse would come in from time to time and ask me how I felt and if I had gone to the bathroom yet? I'd tell her, "No, I haven't gone yet." After several times of the same scenario, I told her that I thought I was ready for seconds! She said she never heard of anyone asking for seconds! I could not help but laugh at her because of the deer caught in the headlight expression on her face! I finally felt the urge and used the bathroom as I was instructed. Once back on the table lying on my side, a team of doctors and nurses came in and stuck a probe with a camera on it, up my butt! They were watching on a TV screen as they moved the probe around inside me. I could feel every little movement and it felt uncomfortable. After a while I had this uncontrollable urge to fart! I was puckering as hard as I could to keep the fart inside! Finally, I asked if they were blowing air in there? The doctor said, "Yes, I need to inflate the intestines to be able to move the probe around." I said, "That's all I needed to know, look out!" and at that instant, I blew a huge fart right in their faces! The group reeled back as if an atomic stink bomb had exploded! They were coughing and fanning the air with their hands! What a day at the doctor's office!

THE DITCH WITCH

When I was building my house, I needed to dig trenches to lay in my waterlines to the house and outside frost proof faucet. My neighbor Ralph B. worked in Cincinnati at the Bobcat Equipment Company where he was able to borrow and bring home any of their equipment that he wanted to use if the equipment was not in use at the time. Usually, he could keep equipment to use over the weekend. It was nice of Ralph to offer the use of a Ditch Witch to dig the trenches for the waterlines. Ralph had a little Isuzu Pup pickup truck that he drove back and forth to work every day. He said the trencher would fit in the back of his truck very easily and he would bring one home for the weekend. When the weekend came, Ralph drove in with the trencher in the back of his truck and the cutting arm with all the blades, which are shaped like small sharp shovel heads, protruding over the cab of his truck. Ralph said let me show you how to operate this thing. I said well let's unload it first. He said no that it wasn't necessary and he could show me how to operate it while it was sitting right there in the truck. I said aren't you afraid it would damage your truck if it got out of control? Ralph said no it's perfectly safe. I said okay go ahead and show me how it works. At that point Ralph started up the trencher and it promptly chewed its way right through the cab roof of his truck!!! Looking in shock and disbelief Ralph shut it off just before it cut down to the rear window and windshield. I remarked to Ralph," I told you we should have unloaded it first!" I think he was still in shock because he didn't know what to reply back to me. Finally, he just blew it off by saying, "Oh, I can fix that with no problem!" I said, "Sure you can!" Then we laughed ourselves silly!

THE ERRAND

I was sitting in my living room one freezing cold winter's day, watching television, when the doorbell rang. When I answered the door, I discovered it was my neighbor Pat. Pat was a little older than myself and was retired. As I opened the door, he asked me for a ride to the filling station up the street. He looked a little cold and tired out, so I told him that I would be glad to give him a ride. As we rode along up the street, he told me that he had locked his keys in his car at the filling station and it was running! He had to come home to get his spare set of keys so he could get into his car. As we reached the stop light at the end of the street, he told me to turn left and keep going. We passed several local filling stations to my surprise and continued across the interstate another mile, to the filling station where his car sat running. That was a several miles walk for him to get home and get his spare keys! I knew Pat had once been a leader in the Boy Scouts and as he exited my car, thanking me for the ride, I jokingly told him that he might have qualified for hiking merit badge! Upon hearing that, he gave me a big smile. That's what life is all about, giving a helping hand to someone in need. It generates a little self-satisfaction, and everyone needs a little of that once in a while.

THE GREAT HORNED OWL

I t was a typical late August morning in the early 1960's and squirrel season was open. I like to check out new places to hunt especially when the hunting is not doing well in the places where I usually go. I had been admiring a wooded area across the valley where I had never been hunting before and it looked like a good place to explore. It was a long way to reach it and it would take a while to cross the creek and climb the hill to get there, but it would be worth it if I could bag a few squirrels there. It had been a dry spring and we had not gotten enough rain to make the nut bearing trees produce nuts. Once in a while you might find a tree near a stream that got enough water to have a few nuts on it and the squirrels would be there in numbers because that was one of the few food sources in the woods. When I reached the top of the wooded ridge, I found that the trees there had no nuts there either. There were plenty of oaks and hickories, but still no nuts. I thought I might as well do some exploring around and see if it's worth coming back next year to hunt here. I could hear some crows of in the distance raising hell with some poor owl. I wondered how close I could get to the action without being seen to see what's going on. There were no squirrels where I was so I might as well sneak up on the crow fight and see how the owl is making out. I was getting pretty close when all of a sudden, the owl must have seen me and came flying over to me and lit on a tree branch above me with about 30 or 40 crows right on his tail! They were screaming, diving and pecking at the big owl. I looked up at him sitting on that limb and couldn't help but feel that the odds were a little unfair. There was one crow that was on the same limb getting right in the owl's face, screaming and pecking at him. I thought maybe the owl could use a little help. I slowly raised my gun and drew a bead on the sassy crow and squeezed the trigger. The crow was killed instantly and the rest of them left out of there in a flash as the dead crow hit the ground. The Great Horned Owl just sat there. Finally, he looked down at me as if to acknowledge a thanks and then flew away. Crows and owls have always been enemies, but for some reason I can't explain, I've always felt good about shooting that crow.

THE INTERVIEW

A friend of mine talked me into joining the Eagles. The Eagles is a very prestigious organization and they screen prospective members before they are allowed to join. They like to know what kind of a person is applying for membership in their organization. My friend told me I would get a phone call from a member of the Eagles organization for an interview. I soon received a phone call from a representative of the Eagles organization and he wanted to interview me. He told me he wanted to know what kind of a person I was and to tell him a little bit about myself. There was a brief moment of hesitation on my part because I have never before been posed a question in that manner. How do you tell someone about the kind of person you are without giving it some serious thought before speaking? At first it seemed it to be a difficult question, but then I thought to say that I am trustworthy, loyal, helpful, friendly, courteous, kind, obedient, cheerful, thrifty, brave, clean and reverent. I'm an Eagle Scout and that is the Scout Law! Those two sentences wrapped up the interview in short order! Without hesitation, I was accepted into the Eagles organization and I soon learned what a great bunch of people I would be associating with. It's a great organization to be associated with and be part of. I think anyone would do well to join an organization of similar structure.

THE LIGHTHOUSE PAINTING

M y wife and I have a house in Johannesburg, Michigan. We like to go there on holidays and spend as much time as we can there. We like to invite friends and relatives to come and stay there with us on certain holidays. When we acquired the house, it was mostly furnished. As time went on we replaced some of the furniture that we did not like or that simply did not fit in with the motif of the house. One of these items was a painting of a lighthouse. It was a strange painting. It was shiny and colorful and glowed in the dark, so to say. It just didn't fit in, so I took it down and placed it in my van. My intention was to take it home and just get rid of it. Our son-in-law, daughter and the grandkids had accompanied us on this particular trip. We were unloading our vans and putting things away after we returned home, when I came across the painting of the lighthouse that I had previously put in my van, while we were in Michigan. Everyone was in the house at that moment, so I thought I would have a little fun and put the painting in their van. Later, while they were unloading their van, at their home, they discovered the painting and called me on the phone. I was told I forgot my painting and that somehow it turned up in their van! I said, no, that I did not forget the painting. I put it there on purpose as a surprise gift! Our daughter did not want it so she brought it back to our house the next time she visited us. The next time we visited them at their house, I sneaked the painting into one of her rooms and sat it up on a shelf for them to eventually discover! Nothing was said, but the next time they visited us, we discovered it sitting somewhere in our house! Well! Game on! I placed it somewhere else in her house for her to discover. The next thing I know, I find it back in my house! Again, I hide it back in her house! This went on for several more times, until one day, I receive a package in the mail at work. I wonder. Who could be sending me a package? As the secretary at the front desk is handing me the package, she remarks that, whatever is in there, must be broken from the sound of it. I open the package and I discover the picture of the lighthouse. It was well padded and wrapped to ensure its safe arrival, but the postal people destroyed it from rough handling, even though it was marked fragile and contained glass. The broken glass had cut the painting all to pieces! End of game! She was sorry and thought it would be a good joke on me, after I told her what had happened to the painting. I told her she should have insured it for $1000. Then the joke would have been on the Post Office!

THE MONEY GUN

A friend of mine, Bill R. was on his way to Tennessee to buy a coon dog. Bill is a professional truck driver and a coon dog enthusiast. Buying and breeding coon dogs can be a very expensive hobby. I guess Bill has always been a coon hunter since he was a boy growing up in southern Indiana. It was not unusual for Bill to travel long distances to look at and by dogs that he thought would make or produce good hunting dogs. While he was on his way to Tennessee to purchase a particular dog, he stopped at a truck stop for a meal and to get his pickup truck washed. As he emerged from the truck wash, a police officer was waiting for him. As Bill rolled down his window, the police officer asked if he could spare a few minutes to talk and would he pull his truck over to the side, out of the way? Bill told him that would be no problem and did as he was asked to do. The police officer then confronted him and wanted to know why he had $5000 in cash in his truck? Bill asked the officer how he could possibly know that he had that amount of money in his truck. The officer then produced a scanning gun like you see in a store for scanning bar codes that had a screen on it. He pointed it at the truck and pulled the trigger. The screen showed that he had $5000 plus the cash in Bill's wallet. Bill asked how does that work and the police officer told him that it reads the magnetic strips in the paper currency that it detects. He said the scanning gun could find money hidden in walls and floors and attics during searches as well as in automobiles. The officer then told him they were having a drug bust at the truck stop and were arresting anyone who had over $2000 cash in their possession. Bill told him he was on his way to Tennessee to buy a coon dog from a local sheriff that he knew. Another police officer on the scene, knew that particular sheriff and verified, Bill's explanation to be true and okay let him go on his way. I thought that was very interesting because I worked for a company that built police equipment and I never heard of such a tool. Another tool that I knew the police do have available to them, is a cup shaped lens that you put over the peephole in motel room doors that reverses the peephole lens, enabling them to see into motel rooms. I think that would be a real fun tool to have!

THE MOON

Have you ever given any thought to what effect the moon has on the planet Earth? The moon is not a planet, it is a star. The moon is the closest star to the planet Earth. The gravitational pull of the moon is what causes the ocean's tide to rise and fall or come in and out, per say, every six hours known as a 12-hour cycle. Have you ever looked at the moon and wondered whether it is on its way toward the moon or is it on its way toward new Moon? The best way to tell which way the moon is going is to notice which side of the moon has the shadow on it or is not filled in, per say. If the left side of the moon is not filled in, is moving toward full moon. If the right side of the moon is not filled in then it is moving toward new Moon. Knowing what the moon is doing has a great bearing on whether my hunting wild game will be a success or not. The moon has a great bearing on the activities of most all animals. Some animals are more active during a full moon while others are less active and vise-versa. I always hunt by the moon and keep close tabs on it. It's amazing how a full moon will light up the landscape as good as daytime when there is a couple of inches of snow on the ground. I find that it is very exhilarating to be out in the woods during this time. It's a shame that people who live in the big cities will probably never get to experience these things, that's what's great about being a member of a youth group such as the Boy Scouts or Girl Scouts, you get to experience a bigger piece of life's wonders.

THE OMEN

No Richard Block before me has ever lived past the age of 52. 52 seems to be some sort of milestone in my family. My grandfather died at 52. My father died at 52. My mother died at 52. I seem to be breaking records because I am 68 at this point in time. My son invited me to go elk hunting high in the Rocky Mountains in Colorado. I have been to Colorado before, and I knew those mountains to be pretty rugged country. I thought it would be a nice adventure, but I wasn't sure if I really wanted to go there. The hunt would take place in late October and it would be hard telling what the weather would be. I happened to stop in the local library where my friend Roy L. is the local historian for one of my usual visits. When I walked through the door, Roy said that he had found something I should see! He went over to the screen where he views old documents and newspapers and brought up a picture of a 1946 local newspaper. On the front page of the paper was an article that said, Richard Block Dies Suddenly. It went on to say that he was hunting with his son, Richard, when he suffered a heart attack and died instantly. The article was about my grandfather and my dad! He was 52 years old. Here I am, contemplating a hunting trip with my son in the Colorado Rockies at an altitude starting at 8000 feet and going up. The air at 8000 feet is pretty thin, let alone at higher altitudes! I'm thinking, what an omen this newspaper article is! Maybe I shouldn't go. I told this to my doctor, and he said that I was worried about nothing and that I should go. He prescribed some pills for me to take if I found that the air was too thin and if I was having difficulty breathing. I'd never heard of such pills for air depravity and anyone I told about them, never heard of them either! I found myself taking deep breaths frequently, but I never resorted to taking any of the pills. We were a party of eight and there was a party of five camped next to us. As luck would have it, one of the hunters in the neighboring hunting party shot an elk. He stayed with the elk while the other hunters brought their guns back to camp and prepared to go back and drag the elk out. When they returned, they found their friend lying face down beside the elk. He had suffered a heart attack and died. He was 52 years old! I guess lightning missed me and struck the camp next door! Déjà vu!

THE PITCH

You are probably thinking about baseball at this moment when the word pitch comes to mind. There are different kinds of pitches that do not involve a ball. The pitch I am referring to is a verbal pitch, such as the pitch a salesman would give when he is trying to sell something. I had the opportunity to travel to Las Vegas, Nevada, to pitch my book to movie producers, at a Pitch Fest. It took place at Caesar's Palace and I was competing against 104 other authors, who were pitching their books also. The purpose is to present your book in a manner that compels the moviemakers to make a movie of your book. There were seminars that I had to attend where we authors were taught and practiced, how to pitch a book. We were allowed 2 minutes, maximum, to present our book pitch to our teacher, who would advise us how to improve our pitches and keep them within the two-minute limit, which is important. I had two different time periods in two different locations, to pitch my book. Each location had seven tables with one or two representatives at each table. They would grade you on your pitch quality and write down whether they were interested in your book as a possible movie prospect. If the producers were interested in a book, they would request a copy from the publisher to read. I had one request for my book, which is more than most of the other authors received. We were advised that it may take a couple of years before any notice is given about making a movie from any book. I really did not expect a lot to come forth from the book pitching adventure, but I enjoyed the experience of meeting other authors and talking with them about their books. It gave me an insight into the world of publishing books and what inspired the authors to write them. Publishing a book is a very expensive venture. You start out by paying the publisher for different services and advertisement programs. It takes a long time and a lot of advertisement to get a book made known to the public, who will purchase your book and earn you royalties for your investments. I am constantly asked, what inspired me to write a book. I have to answer that by saying that I just want to make a person's life a little better, by them learning things about life that they should be experiencing for themselves and maybe finding a little humor among the pages to brighten their day as well. I get a lot of great feedback about my stories. It gives me a good feeling to know that everyone who has read my book, has enjoyed it immensely and that is my goal.

THE PURSE

Once upon a time, as the story goes, I had a small percentage ownership in a strip mall. One of the chores my wife and I would perform was to go there on a weekend and pick up the trash from the parking lot and do a little landscaping. When I went to the dumpster to deposit some trash, I noticed a woman's purse in the bottom of the dumpster, with all the contents spilled out. I knew something was wrong because you just do not throw away something with all those personal items in it. I thought to myself, I wonder where the woman is that owns the purse. Maybe she is in one of the other dumpsters in the area. So, I called the police and asked them to send an officer to where I would be waiting. In the meantime, I climbed into the dumpster and gathered up all of the materials that obviously came from within the purse. The ladies driver's license, credit cards, her children's birth certificates from the state of Tennessee and other important documents that should be kept in a safe place and not in a purse were all there! I found no money nor any phone number. The driver's license was from Ohio and had a local address on it. When the officer arrived, I gave him the purse and told him the story behind it. I had looked in the dumpsters around the mall and found nothing else to indicate where the woman was. We had shared the story with our daughter who lives in the area and as luck would have it, she knew someone who knew this particular lady by being her neighbor. The message was passed on to her that her purse had been found and it was at the police station. It was two or three days before the police notified her that they had her purse. The story came back to me that the lady and her family had been dining at one of the local restaurants late in the evening and left at closing time. She promptly remembered her purse and returned to the restaurant to retrieve it. She and the manager searched throughout the restaurant but could find no purse. The manager suspected one of the employees probably had taken it. She said there was only five dollars in cash in it and she canceled the credit cards the following morning. I can only hope she learned an important lesson about where to keep precious documents! I think the employee was let go a few days later. So much for honesty, I guess.

THE RAILROAD CROSSING

We were getting ready for a Boy Scout camp out on a Friday afternoon, and I was one of the adult leaders. We met at the Boy Scout cabin in the Aurora city Park and loaded our cars up with all of our gear. I was 18 at the time and I was driving my 1953 Chevrolet that had once belonged to my grandmother. The campout was going to be held in Batesville, Indiana at camp Mesty, which was near Margaret Mary Hospital. Our scoutmaster, Buck Crontz, was driving his old blue 1955 Chevrolet that he always drove us boys around in, everywhere we went. This was a typical campout, and I was following behind Buck as we headed to Batesville. Buck worked for the railroad and he seemed to be able to spend the time needed to be a good scoutmaster. As we came into the town of Sunman, the lights started flashing at the railroad crossing ahead of us. I stopped my car back a distance from the railroad crossing, leaving a couple of car spaces between Buck's car and mine. It seemed to me that he was unusually close to the railroad tracks at the crossing. As the train came closer, the barrier arms came down and with a whacking sound, landed on the hood of

Buck's car! The barrier then raised up a couple of feet and came down, whacking on the hood of Buck's car again! As the barrier raised again, Buck backed his car up into the spaces I had provided for him and then stopped as the barrier arm came completely down and sat into place. Buck jumped out of his car and came back to where I sat parked. He had a somewhat embarrassed look on his face as he told me, "Don't you ever tell anyone what you just saw happen!" Many years later, we were having a "Buck Roast" at one of our district dinners and the story of the railroad crossing was told on him by another member who I had put up to telling it. Buck immediately jumped up and asked," How did you get that story?" Everyone was too busy laughing to really care. He was a great man and is missed by many men my age who were scouts in his troop.

THE SAFE

B rett, a friend of mine was at an auction and he thought things were going fairly cheap and that I was missing out on a lot of bargains, so he called me on the phone and told me that I should come there as soon as I could. The man who owned the property had died previously and his relatives were settling the estate and most of his possessions. He was not married and had a lifetime of collections of guns, knives, ammunition and many other items. When I arrived and met up with Brett, the auctioneer was standing on a flatbed farm wagon auctioning items that were piled all around him. The auctioneer did not know very much about the items he was selling, so he had no idea of what their value was. I felt things were selling too cheap, so I moved up close to him and advised him as to what he was selling when he would pick up an item and put it up for bid. Things started moving along much better, because the people knew more about what they were bidding on. The auctioneer had no idea what the ammunition was that he was selling. I would tell him what caliber they were and what country it was made in. Among some of the items sitting around the auction wagon platform, were some safes. Some of them were large gun safes that had the combinations with them, and they sold at a good price. There were some smaller safes that had no combinations, and no one would bid on them because of that. One of the small safes was unlocked and the door was open. I bid two dollars on the open safe and got it for that price. I was the only bidder. I had experience with changing safe combinations when I was a manager at McDonald's. I knew that if the door was open on a safe you would be able to find out the combination or change it to a new one. I took the safe home and lifted the door of the safe from its hinges, which is a simple thing to do. I then took the door to a friend of mine who is a locksmith and had him find out what the combination was. He charged be $35 and I now had a working safe! I thought I did pretty well because I now had a safe worth $200 that I only had a total of $37 invested in! Sometimes auction items work out well and sometimes they do not. They did not auction any guns there that day because the man's relatives kept them all. I have been to auctions where guns are on the menu and people get into a buying frenzy and usually pay more for a fairly new gun than you can buy it cheaper for at a gun shop!

TONY DELUCO

Tony was a first-generation Italian. His wife Bert was a first-generation German. How they met and got married, I never inquired. Tony was a welder and owned his own weld shop on Glenway Avenue in Cincinnati. His wife Bert answered the phone and kept the books, while his two sons Tony junior and Joe, worked in the shop. I used them frequently to repair broken items from McDonald's restaurants. I was constantly taking French fry baskets to Tony, to get the handles welded. There was a multitude of other things as well. When I started out at McDonald's as a manager trainee, Tony's shop was next door to the restaurant and that's how I came to know Tony and his family. They rented out the top of their building to a camera shop which had a small strip of grass in front of the building, between the sidewalk and the curb. When we mowed our grass at the restaurant, I always mowed the grass in front of Tony's building also. They never asked me to mow it, but I knew they appreciated it. Whenever I walked in with something that needed welding, they would usually weld it immediately and I could take it with me, repaired and ready to return to the restaurant. Tony's shop also manufactured wrought iron railings for porches and stair steps at residences. Tony's son Joey, designs and manufactures custom furniture made of wrought iron for displays in large department stores. Tony was very talented. He used to go to the old folks' homes and play his electric accordion on the weekends for their entertainment. I had a project for Tony over at the boss's house one day. I wanted some wrought iron gates on hinges and wheels that would close off the entryway into the boss's house which had a tile floor. When the gates were closed it formed an area to keep the boss's dog contained in. We called it the jail. While Tony was installing the gates, he noticed the boss had a grand piano. He asked the boss if he played the piano and the boss said that he did. Tony said he would like to hear him play something and maybe they could play a gig together sometime. The boss sat down and started playing his piano and Tony said, "Oh, you are one of those doodley do players and I can't use you!" The boss was a concert pianist and didn't play the kind of music Tony plays. I thought it was hilarious when he made that statement to the boss! It's not often you get to see your boss be insulted in a funny way! The look on the boss's face was a real Kodak moment.

TRAVEL OVERNITE

When I travel, I like to travel overnight. I'm a night person anyhow and when I travel overnight, I am not wasting an entire day to cover the same ground. On a trip that takes 7 to 8 hours travel time, I can leave at five or six in the evening and get there around 2 o'clock in the morning which leaves me plenty of time to sleep and be able to get up and start my day at my new destination. It's like not having any traveling time at all. The time that I am traveling is usually the time that I am watching TV until all hours of the morning. All I am really sacrificing is a little TV time! Returning home is a different story. I usually stay until three or four in the afternoon before leaving so I can make it home just before midnight. That way I can get a full night's sleep before going to work the next day. Again, I have only sacrificed a little TV time. The great thing about traveling at night is that there is less traffic and it's moving faster, plus the road signs are illuminated, which makes them easier to see. Traveling in this manner gives me an extra day and a half of time at my original destination. I rarely travel alone. On a rare occasion where I might get tired of driving, I have someone with me who can drive while I take a nap! If you do some traveling or are taking a vacation, you should try this method. I highly recommend it.

TURTLE SURPRISE

We were on one of our Boy Scout trips to Michigan, where we spend a week camping, canoeing and seeing the sights. Sometimes we go to Mackinac Island and let the boys loose for the day to explore the island and learn its history. The boat ride out to the island is something everyone looks forward to. It's a fun trip zooming across Lake Huron on a jet boat headed to the island and experiencing the spray from the waves hitting you in the face if you are up on the top deck! I prefer to sit inside and watch the water spray, wash the windows! We always like to visit the local scout camp west of Grayling when we are in the area and this was no exception on this particular trip. I was driving our troop bus down the sandy road that led to the scout camp which is named Camp Tapico, an abbreviation for Tall Pines Council. Sitting close to me was the Go-fer. The go-fer's job is to "go for" whatever I see along the road and bring it back to me on the bus. Well on this sunny day I happened to spot a rather large soft-shell turtle crossing the road. I stopped the bus and yelled "fetch" to the Go-fer as I opened the bus's door. A lucky scout by the name of Troy was today's Go-fer, so up he jumped and out the door he went! He had no idea what he was after until he spied the big fat turtle. He ran over to it and snatched it up in short order. Upon climbing back aboard the bus, the boys were all curious and yelling, "Hold it up Troy and show us what you got!" At that, he held the turtle up high over his head so everyone could see which happened to be the very same moment that the turtle let go a giant stream of pee, the likes of which I had never before seen! It was as if someone had turned on a faucet of water, giving Troy the shower of his life! The scouts were screaming laughing and rolling around in the isles! It was so unexpected that I couldn't keep from laughing either, even though I felt a little sorry for Troy. He was a good sport of a scout.

VISITORS FROM ABROAD

McDonald's regional office in Columbus Ohio, phoned our McDonald's of greater Cincinnati office, requesting the use of our company motor coach and driver. The head of all the McDonald's restaurants in Sweden was going to be here with a group of people, to tour some of the restaurants and building sites under construction, in our area. They were here to learn how we build our current McDonald's restaurants here in America. Paul L. was the Swedish McDonald's president and he spoke very good English. His group consisted of a woman and two other men, who spoke some or no English at all. These people were contractors and electricians here to take pictures and gather samples of materials, used in the construction of our McDonald's here in America. They were expanding their operations in Sweden, to the suburbs away from the city. In Europe, you are not allowed to change the architecture of the face of a building. You can change or remodel anything inside, but the outside must remain historically the same. Now that they were beginning to move from the city, they could build standard McDonald's restaurants, which was something new to them. As I took the group from place to place, they took roll after roll of 35mm camera film and gathered samples of different types of building materials which included tile. I hurried them along as best as I could, because I wanted to make a stop that was not on their schedule. We were going to be touring in the area of our newly constructed Ronald McDonald House that was now in operation. I phoned our operations assistant, Karen B. and had her set up a tour of the Ronald McDonald House, with the house manager. As we got close to our next touring site, I told the group we were going to make an unscheduled stop of interest, as I pulled up in front of the Ronald McDonald House. We unloaded and went inside where I introduced them to the house manager. She gladly toured them through the house and explained how it operated. The group was unusually silent as they took the tour. I later found out that Paul L. had a child that has the same problem as some of the children staying there. The Ronald McDonald House was still a new concept and had not reached Sweden yet, but I could see that they really related to ours here. After all of the touring was finished, we assembled with McDonald's corporate personnel at the Golden Lamb restaurant in Lebanon, Ohio for an evening dinner. As the dinner meeting came to a close, Paul L. thanked everyone and being that they had asked so many questions of us, did we have any questions for them? Everyone seemed stupefied except for me. I said, "Yes I have a few questions." "What is the minimum wage in Sweden?" "How how much does a gallon of gas cost there?" "What is the best-selling item on your menu?" Paul answered every question in detail. It was interesting to learn that the soft serve ice cream cone was their best-selling item and that their currency was crowns and not dollars. Paul must have been impressed with me, because he sent me a book about Sweden and invited me to come and visit. That was over 30 years ago, but I still relish the invitation!

VOLKSWAGEN

I lived on Market Street, which was located on a steep hill overlooking the Ohio River. My friend Reggie and I had been on top of the hill and we were returning to my house. Reggie was driving his Dad's VW minibus as we came down the steep street. All of a sudden, a kid on a minibike darted out into the street from between two parked cars! Reggie jerked the steering wheel to the right and the VW bus instantly darted to the right, missing the kid on the minibike. I could hardly believe what I had just seen! How did he miss hitting that kid? If I had been driving, that kid would have been a hood ornament! Reggie's quick reaction and the instant response of the Volkswagen saved that boy from serious injury or maybe death. I gained a new respect for Volkswagens that day. I had always thought that because they were such a small car, a person was more at risk of getting killed in an accident. So, I started looking around in the junk yards to see how many smashed-up Volkswagens were there and I found that there were very few and the ones that I did find were there because of motor issues. Impressive, I thought. It wasn't long before I found myself owning a VW bug. I soon learned after driving it for a while and learning it's capabilities that the reason there were not many smashed up VW's in the junk yards was because they could out maneuver the big slow American cars. I proved this one day on my way to work. It had been raining earlier and there were large water puddles on the roads. I was going east on a 4-lane highway with a concrete divider separating the 4 lanes in the middle. There was a big Ford full size car traveling west at a pretty fast rate of speed and upon hitting a large puddle of water, it started water planning and jumping up and down and started to turn sideways! I had just left the stop light going east and I was out front with a group of cars behind me. I thought, I am glad that concrete divider is there and at that instant, the big Ford Sedan jumped the divider and came straight at me sideways with nowhere to go! It was like slow motion. I turned my wheel to the right and my little VW hopped the curb onto the grass zipped around the Ford and out of harm's way, leaving him to go crashing into the traffic behind me. I went about a ¼ mile before I pulled back upon the highway. I never looked back to see what happened. I was just thankful that my little car could run circles around those big slower cars. Sometime later I lost my little car to a drunk driver who came home sober for once and left his car roll down the street smashing my car in the rear and shoving it into a telephone pole, crushing it to pieces. I always thought that if he had been in his usual state of drunkenness, there probably would have been no problem! A sad end for such a fun car!

WALMART

Sam Walton was an amazing man. When he retired from his job in a hardware store, he swore he would start a business and put Kmart out of business. He started his Walmart store, and it grew into the multi- million-dollar business that it is today. I'm sure he never dreamed that it would grow to be so big! The selection of items in his stores is so large that you can find everything you need in a one shop stop! There is no need to go anywhere else! I get these emails all the time that are titled walmartians, that show Walmart shoppers dressed in the most outrageous clothing you can imagine or even the lack of clothing as well! When my wife goes shopping there, I usually sit on one of the benches by the end of the checkout line where I can watch the shoppers check out while I wait for my wife. I get worn out just walking around the store. It's so big anymore. If you want to see people that you haven't seen in a long time, that's the place to go and meet them! Different organizations often sell things or seek donations in front of their entrance doors. You have to apply for a date and time for your organization to be there at their entrance. There are so many organizations that want to sell things or seek donations that it is hard to get a scheduled time to be there. A friend of mine told me once that if you want to see a lot of good-looking women, just hang out at the grocery store! I guess that's why I always ran into him there! I was at Walmart the other day and I saw a young man by a life preserver that you wear on a boat. He must've been very proud of it because he was wearing it as he left the store! Every time I hear some kid crying out loud, I say that's the way my wife acts when I tried to get her out of Walmart!

WATER

I t is hard to conceive, just how valuable water is, to our way of life. For most people, it is something you take for granted, you just turn the valve and it comes out! In the western part of the United States, water is as valuable as gold! You have to have water to sustain life. I am speaking of potable water of course. By the term, potable, I mean drinkable, water that is safely consumed by human beings. Even though the earth is mostly covered by water, the majority of it is saltwater, which is not consumable without desalination. We are lucky here in our country, because we have a good supply of freshwater. The majority of people, here, depend on city water, which is piped into their homes from a water purification plant. When I bought my farm, my only water supply was a well. My well produced good water, but it was not enough to last throughout the year without running dry. In the hot and dry months of August and September, I would have to buy a truck load of water occasionally and dump it down the well, to be able to have a water supply. I applied for water from the local water company, but a large demand for the city water would have to be established in my area before the running of any waterlines would be considered. A federal grant would also have to be applied for, to help cover the cost of the pipeline construction. The water company wanted a $100 deposit up front, just to put me on the list of people, who would like water piped to their residences. They could not guarantee any time lapse before the water would be supplied. I went to some of the Water Board meetings and discovered that there were people who had put down deposits, years ago and still had not received water yet. I told them I was not going to put a $100 deposit down without some guarantee of delivery. To make a long story short, it took 20 years to finally receive city water. I had to a grant right of **way**, for the water company to bury their pipeline across my property, as well as the other property owners in my area had to do the same. It cost $200, to tap into the new pipeline and have a meter installed for each person, wanting the city water. I convinced the water company to put a fire hydrant on my property, near, where my meter was located. From the meter, which was a quarter of a mile away, it was my responsibility to bury the connecting pipeline, from there, to my house. I had to hire an individual contractor, to do this and it was not cheap! As soon as everything was in good, operating order, I called my insurance company and told them about the fire hydrant beside my driveway. They instantly, cut my insurance premiums in half, due to that fact. I remember years before, when my neighbor's house caught fire. Even though he had a pond next to his house, the fire department would not pump water from it, for fear of getting mud in their fire trucks pump! As a result, his house burned to the ground while the firemen watched! It kind of makes you thankful for what you have, doesn't it?cost, to bury the additional

WILEY COYOTE

One November day, I was deer hunting on my friend Phil Weaver's farm, where I have hunted since I was a boy. The land there is all hills and some of them are fairly steep. On top of the hill are power lines that run for miles. I always liked to hunt along these power lines because they are an open clear area that is great for spotting game. One day I was climbing one of the steep hills along the power lines looking for deer and as I approached the top of the hill, I crouched down and rose up slowly to peak over the top of the ridge to see if there was anything on the other side. To my surprise, I saw a coyote coming my way. I thought to myself that this will be a good opportunity to shoot a coyote. All I have to do is sit tight and wait for him to top the rise where I will be waiting for him on the other side. I crouched back down below the ridge and waited. It seemed like it was taking him forever to get there so I thought I would take another peek. I slowly rose up again to peek over the ridge and the coyote was right there doing the same thing! There we were nose to nose, to both of our surprise! The coyote turned around and took off running, looking over his shoulder at me as he ran. I couldn't shoot at him because I was laughing too hard! I thought that if there had been an obstacle in his way, he would've ran right into it because he was too busy looking behind him as he ran! You know, you don't have to shoot something every time you go hunting. Sometimes you get more enjoyment out of just experiencing the outdoors.

WIND

Have you ever thought about the wind? What causes the wind? How and why does it blow? It always seems like on a hot summer's day when you could use a nice breeze, you rarely get one! In the winter, when you don't need a breeze, that's when you get the ones that chill you to the bone! I made the comment one time that I like to pour concrete in the late afternoon because the leaves do not fall off the trees after dark. The person I told that to said that they did not believe that. I explained it's because the wind stops blowing in the evening and the trees are calm, that's why the leaves do not fall and get into my wet concrete. As the summer progresses into fall, the wind blows less of a morning and less in early evening unless a storm is coming. I always enjoyed visiting my in-laws in Valparaiso, Indiana in the winter. The winter winds blow there because they are close to the Great Lakes. I used to lie in bed at night and listen to the wind whistling at the windows, it was like a lullaby. Their second floor was not heated, and it was ice cold as well. Those are good memories of places and people long gone. You don't realize how much you miss those things until you think of them.

In mid August, the winds are usually calm in the mornings during squirrel hunting season. Sometimes the dew is heavy and dripping from the tree leaves. It makes it hard to tell where the squirrels are unless they jump on a tree limb and shake the dew from the leaves. About 10:00 AM, the wind will pick up and it sounds like it's raining but it's just the dew falling from the trees. When you're around the ocean, the wind is always blowing night and day. I miss the smell of the salt air and the feel of the ocean breeze on my body. I could do without the sand though! It's hard to walk in at times and wears me out. Besides, sand gets into everything! Sand is one of the oldest materials on earth. Each grain of sand is millions of years old! It's really amazing, this planet earth we live on!

ABOUT THE AUTHOR

Colonel Richard W. Block is an Eagle Scout and a Scouter for 50 years, an avid sportsman, an instructor for the Department of Wildlife, a Fourth Degree Knight, N.R.A. Life Member and Certified Instructor and works with the parents of West Point Cadets of Indian.